DATE DUE

EATING DISORDERS
WHEN FOOD IS AN OBSESSION

By Kristen Rajczak Nelson

Portions of this book originally appeared in *Eating Disorders* by Toney Allman.

Published in 2017 by
Lucent Press, an Imprint of Greenhaven Publishing, LLC
353 3rd Avenue
Suite 255
New York, NY 10010

Designer: Seth Hughes
Editor: Jennifer Lombardo

Cataloging-in-Publication Data

Names: Rajczak Nelson, Kristen.
Title: Eating disorders: when food Is an obsession / Kristen Rajczak Nelson.
Description: New York : Lucent Press, 2017. | Series: Hot topics| Includes index.
Identifiers: ISBN 9781534560147 (library bound) | ISBN 9781534560154 (ebook)
Subjects: LCSH: Eating disorders–Juvenile literature.
Classification: LCC RC552.E18 R285 2017 | DDC 616.85'26–dc23

Printed in the United States of America

CPSIA compliance information: Batch #CW17KL: For further information contact Greenhaven Publishing LLC, New York,
New York at 1-844-317-7404.

Please visit our website, www.greenhavenpublishing.com. For a free color catalog of all our high-quality books, call toll free 1-844-317-7404 or fax 1-844-317-7405.

CONTENTS

Adolescence is a time when many people begin to take notice of the world around them. News channels, blogs, and radio talk shows are constantly promoting one view or another; very few are unbiased. Young people also hear conflicting information from parents, friends, teachers, and acquaintances. Often, they will hear only one side of an issue or be given flawed information. People who are trying to support a particular viewpoint may cite inaccurate facts and statistics on their blogs, and news programs present many conflicting views of important issues in our society. In a world where it seems everyone has a platform to share their thoughts, it can be difficult to find unbiased, accurate information about important issues.

It is not only facts that are important. In blog posts, in comments on online videos, and on talk shows, people will share opinions that are not necessarily true or false, but can still have a strong impact. For example, many young adults struggle with their body image. Seeing or hearing negative comments about particular body types online can have a huge effect on the way someone views himself or herself and may lead to depression and anxiety. Although it is important not to keep information hidden from teens under the guise of protecting them, it is equally important to offer encouragement on issues that affect their mental health.

The titles in the Hot Topics series provide young adults with different viewpoints on important issues in today's society. Many of these issues, such as teen pregnancy and Internet safety, are of immediate concern to young people. This series aims to give teens factual context on these crucial topics in a way that lets them form their own opinions. The facts presented throughout also serve to empower readers to help themselves or support people they know who are struggling with many of the challenges adolescents face today. Although negative viewpoints are not ignored or downplayed, this series also focuses on allowing young people to see that the challenges they face are not insurmountable. Eating disorders can be overcome, the Internet can be navigated safely, and pregnant teens do not have to feel hopeless.

Quotes encompassing all viewpoints are presented and cited so teens can trace them back to their original source, verifying for themselves whether the information comes from a reputable place. Additional books and websites are listed, giving readers a starting point from which to continue their own research. Chapter questions encourage discussion, allowing teens to hear and understand their classmates' points of view as they further solidify their own. Full-color photographs and enlightening charts provide a deeper understanding of the topics at hand. All of these features augment the informative text, helping young adults understand the world they live in and formulate their own opinions concerning the best way they can improve it.

Not Another Fad Diet

Eating disorders are difficult to understand. They are often hard to diagnose and not easy to treat, but most of all, they are difficult to live with.

People with eating disorders did not choose to have them. Their problems are not simply a part of fad diets, teenage phases, or a sign of weakness. Eating disorders are dangerous illnesses that cause mental and physical suffering and may have lifelong consequences.

People with eating disorders are unable to use food in a healthy way—as a source of energy and nutrition. They can no longer connect to their body's signals of hunger or fullness. Instead of enjoying school, friends, and sports, they are obsessed with food to the point that their feelings, thoughts, and activities are ruled by stress and worry about themselves and what they eat. Whether starving, compulsively eating, or forcing their bodies to reject food, individuals with eating disorders are trapped in a pattern of unhealthy eating habits and negative self-image.

Most people struggling with eating disorders agree that the illness is not about food and weight. Some people might have certain genes that make them more likely to have an eating disorder, which means these illnesses can run in families. Emotional issues, such as problems with parents, also play a big role in developing an eating disorder. Eating disorders may be symptoms of other psychological troubles, too, such as anxiety or depression. No matter the cause, those who suffer from eating disorders may feel intense self-hate, sadness, and loneliness.

Recovery from an eating disorder means, in large part, facing and dealing with these bad feelings. Although it is painful and frightening, many people with eating disorders are able to find the support they need to work through their food issues, as well as the emotional troubles that may be behind them. They learn to like themselves and work on eating normally again. For

Eating disorders seem to be about food, but more often, they are ways for people to cope with negative emotions.

some, this can take months; for others, years. Still others may never recover.

The good news is that scientists, researchers, and mental health professionals around the world are studying eating disorders to find more effective ways of treating and preventing them. In order to fight back, those who suffer from eating disorders, as well as their friends and family, need to arm themselves with information from these experts. By using the latest research and considering the experiences of those with eating disorders, we can begin to understand the complex problem of eating disorders many teens face.

What Is an Eating Disorder?

In 2013, Amalie Lee was seriously underweight. Her health was declining so rapidly that she could no longer ride a bike for fear of injury if she fell. The year before, Lee had been diagnosed with anorexia nervosa, an eating disorder, but she did not seek help until she realized her health was at stake. Lee was constantly tired, cold, and stressed from all the food rules she had made for herself. She withdrew from her life. As she told the *Today* show in 2015: "I would just live in my own little bubble. I lost a lot of friends and the friends that I kept, I didn't want to talk to."[1]

Like many people with eating disorders, Lee did not always look unhealthy on the outside. Inside, Lee was hurting: "My eating disorder was triggered by depression but then I started to eat less and lose weight and I just ended up in a spiral that just went downwards."[2] However, by 2013, she knew something had to change. Looking back, Lee said, "The thought of spending the rest of my life alone, utterly consumed by an illness, eventually became more frightening than the thought of recovery."[3] Lee entered a recovery program and began documenting her journey back to health on Instagram and a blog called *Let's Recover*, which serve as places for her to speak to others going through the tough recovery process.

Not everyone who suffers from an eating disorder is able to see his or her problem as clearly as Lee eventually did. *Newsweek* reported about Natalya, a young woman who developed anorexia in response to her brother's death. Natalya told *Newsweek*: "It consumed my entire life. Every second of every day, I was thinking about food and how little I could eat and still live."[4]

Eating disorders are seriously abnormal eating patterns that affect physical health. People with eating disorders do not choose to eat too much or too little. They are affected by psychological disorders, which are emotional or mental problems that affect

People who suffer from eating disorders will believe they are fat even when they are not.

thoughts and feelings so that people behave in ways that could harm them. Eating disorders commonly lead to physical and medical issues, which makes eating disorders diseases of the body as well as the mind. The definition used by the National Institute of Mental Health (NIMH) includes "obsessions with food, body weight, and shape"[5] as signs of an eating disorder.

There is a difference between eating disorders and disordered eating. People who try to lose weight by only drinking meal replacement shakes or cutting out whole food groups may have abnormal eating habits, but not an eating disorder. Picky eaters or people who overdo sweet foods do not have eating disorders. Even unusual thinness or being overweight do not necessarily mean a person has an eating disorder. The difference between an extreme dieter and someone with an eating disorder is a truly disordered relationship with food that interferes with everyday life. A dieter may avoid cake at a birthday party in order to lose weight. Someone with an eating disorder may not go to the party at all in order to avoid eating with other people. This is just one example of how someone with an eating disorder is unable to go through normal life when suffering from the disease.

Eating disorders may take different forms, but they are real illnesses in which the victim has a distorted and disordered view of himself or herself. This view leads to unhealthy and dangerous eating habits that the sufferer cannot stop or reverse. Currently, eating disorders fall into three main types defined by certain symptoms and behaviors.

Who Has an Eating Disorder?

Amalie Lee and Natalya are just two of the millions of people ill with eating disorders around the world. According to the NIMH, about 0.1 percent of children in the United States ages 8 to 15 suffer from an eating disorder. That number increases as older teens are included. About 2.7 percent of teens between 13 and 18 have an eating disorder. These numbers clearly show that as the teen years go on, eating disorders become more common. The

Healthy Teen Project, an eating disorder recovery clinic, reports about 95 percent of people with eating disorders are between 12 and 25.

Eating disorders can affect anyone. Both boys and girls can have eating disorders, but girls are more than two-and-a-half times as likely to develop one. Experts say that around the world, eating disorders generally affect young people living in developed countries that have achieved high economic status. Poor people in developing countries who are struggling to find enough food to survive do not develop eating disorders. Within more well-off societies, however, anyone of any class, ethnic group, race, gender, or socioeconomic status can be vulnerable to eating disorders.

What Is Anorexia Nervosa?

Anorexia nervosa is the medical and psychiatric term for the disease of self-starvation. Although it can begin at any age, it typically affects adolescents and young adults. It is commonly estimated that anorexia occurs in about 1 in 100 to 200 young women, and that about 5 to 15 percent of all those suffering from anorexia are young men. However, it is hard to know for sure because it is likely many people do not report their problems.

The name "anorexia nervosa" comes from the Greek words *an*, meaning "without," and *orexis*, meaning "appetite." "Nervosa" means that the brain is involved in the disorder. However, the name, which was coined in the late 1800s, is not completely accurate. People with anorexia actually do have an appetite for food. They are unable to give in to or respond to hunger because of their illness, and instead, they severely limit their food intake. As with other eating disorders, anorexia is not about food. It is about finding a way to work through emotional trials. To someone with anorexia, thinness is equated to worthiness.

The story of one young girl from experts at Harvard's eating disorder treatment center show how these symptoms can arise. Thirteen-year-old Shelley (not her real name) was not overweight, but she decided to go on a diet. As she began to lose weight, she received a lot of praise from friends and family. Soon, they noticed that the weight loss did not stop. Shelley looked skinny and unhealthy, yet her diet became more and more restricted. She started to seem uneasy and anxious during family meals. Her father reported, "Shelley would spread jelly on a slice of toast, scrape it off, and reapply it, repeating this process 15 times before she'd take a bite. It was agonizing to watch. I remember making pancakes for breakfast. Shelley put one on her plate, cut it up into miniscule pieces, and took more than an hour to eat them."[6]

Onset of Eating Disorder

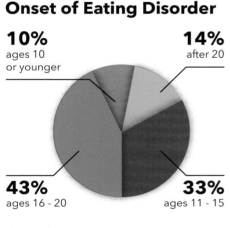

10%
ages 10 or younger

14%
after 20

43%
ages 16 - 20

33%
ages 11 - 15

One in ten are male.

Duration of Illness

1 - 5 years

6 - 10 years

11 - 15 years*

Treatment

Half report being cured, though many continue to display traits of the disorder. An estimated 6 percent die.

* In 23 percent, the duration can be longer.

These statistics from the National Association of Anorexia Nervosa and Associated Disorders reflect the number of people who report having anorexia. Since sufferers of this illness try to keep it a secret, it is difficult to get an exact count.

IT TAKES OVER YOUR LIFE

"Eating disorders demand every second of your attention and take over every aspect of your life. I scheduled my study time immediately after cross-country practice so I wouldn't have time to eat. I avoided my friends at lunch so they wouldn't notice I threw my food away. I cried hysterically when my mom asked me to come down to dinner until she let me stay in my room. The number of things I missed out on because I was afraid of food is actually unbelievable to me now."

—McKenzie Maxon, editorial intern, Greatist

McKenzie Maxson, "The Biggest Misconceptions About Eating Disorders (From Someone Who's Had One)," Greatist, July 13, 2016. greatist.com/live/eating-disorders-myths-to-stop-believing.

Shelley showed her fear of and resistance to weight gain in other ways, too. She began eliminating whole food groups, such as meat and sweets, from her diet. She lied to and tricked her parents about what she had eaten. For instance, she would arrange a bowl with a bit of milk and one or two flakes of cereal in it. She left the bowl on the kitchen counter in an effort to fool her parents into thinking she had eaten breakfast before leaving for school. She always told her parents that she ate at school, while in reality, she was skipping lunch altogether. She stopped going out with friends because their gatherings so often included having a pizza or hamburgers together. When she was forced to sit down at the table with her family, Shelley pretended to eat by raising her filled fork to her mouth, then, when no one was watching, lowering it without taking a bite and moving the food around on her plate.

Those with anorexia commonly lie about how much or what they have eaten. They are so afraid of gaining weight or losing control of their eating behaviors that it can be an unbearable feeling. Despite being semi-starved, people such as Shelley are sure that they are too big. When they look in the mirror, they do not see "skin and bones," but fat. Therefore, they are determined

Sufferers of anorexia may hide their food or throw it away when no one is looking so they can keep their eating disorder a secret.

to deny any type of problem and insist (and believe) that they are eating healthily and need to lose more weight. Their body image, or how they see themselves, is distorted, and because of this, they become more determined to restrict the foods they allow themselves.

How Anorexia Can Harm the Body

Eventually, the types of foods and calories eaten by those with anorexia become so limited that they become seriously malnourished. The meals they eat are so tiny that their bodies cannot grow and develop properly. Their bodies no longer have enough fuel to heal well or stop the damage being done to their organs. Teen girls and women who allow themselves to become this malnourished will experience amenorrhea, or an absence of their period because their body fat is too low for their hormones to work correctly. Amenorrhea can have long-term health consequences on its own, including problems having children later in life.

Lack of menstrual periods, however, is but one of several medical issues caused by anorexia. When the body is starving, the muscles start to waste away since they are not being fed anything to help them grow or get stronger. This is an especially serious problem for an important muscle in the body: the heart. People suffering from anorexia have a lower blood pressure than normal and a heart rate as low as 30 to 40 beats per minute. The normal average is between 60 and 100 beats per minute. Low heart rate and blood pressure can make people dizzy or faint, especially when they stand up. These symptoms may mean the heart is getting weaker. The heart may be harmed so badly by malnutrition that congestive heart failure develops, and death becomes a real possibility.

If a person with anorexia is young enough to still be growing, bone development can be slowed or stopped. Osteoporosis is likely to develop, too. This disease, which generally occurs in the elderly, features a loss of bone density. The thinning of bones leads to an increased risk of breaks in the bone and injuries that can last throughout life.

Osteoporosis

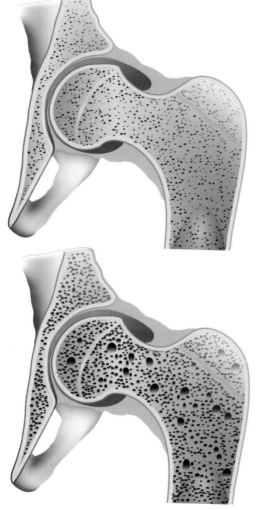

normal bone

bone with
osteoporosis

*The bones of a sufferer of anorexia are often more fragile because he or she
is not taking in enough important nutrients, such as calcium.*

When malnutrition becomes severe, every organ in the body is affected. Metabolism—all the processes of the body that keep a living thing alive—slows down. In the digestive system, the stomach will empty slower and the intestines will not take up nutrients as well or as quickly. People may experience constipation, or a difficulty eliminating waste, and extra gas in their body, or bloating. The brain and nervous system also suffer from malnutrition—it is possible for the brain to shrink in some cases. Someone with anorexia may experience memory loss, problems concentrating, and even seizures. The body becomes unable to maintain a normal temperature, and the person may feel cold all the time. Hands and feet may turn blue. Hair loss and dry, yellow skin are common.

Dangerous heart problems can be made worse by some behaviors people with anorexia use in their quest to lose weight and hide disordered eating patterns from other people. For example, people may use laxatives and diuretics to maintain a low body weight. Laxatives are meant to help people eliminate feces when they are constipated. A person with anorexia may use a lot of them at once to cause diarrhea and supposedly cleanse his or her body of "forbidden" calories. Diuretics, or medicines used for increasing urination, are abused by some people with anorexia in order to get rid of water weight. Excessive use of laxatives and diuretics, however, upsets the body's electrolyte balance. Electrolytes are minerals that help control the balance of fluid and conduct electrical impulses throughout the body. When these chemicals are out of balance, people become dehydrated and fatigued. Their muscles function poorly, and since the heart is a muscle, heart rhythms become abnormal. If a person's heart rate becomes too slow or erratic, their heart can stop altogether and result in death.

In truth, death rates for anorexia are greater than those of any other eating disorder or psychiatric illness. The statistics can be scary. According to the NIMH, almost 10 percent of anorexia sufferers die of complications from the disease or commit suicide. Other mental health problems, such as depression and anxiety, commonly occur alongside anorexia. These problems—particularly depression—can include suicidal thoughts and

Types of Anorexia

Not everyone with anorexia is the same. However, they are generally grouped by how they maintain their low body weight and low calorie consumption. First, there is the restricting type. Those with this kind of anorexia restrict, or set limits to, their food intake. People with restricting type anorexia are those who will skip meals or eat tiny meals, such as a diet soda and carrot sticks for lunch.

Binge/purge type anorexia is another main category. These sufferers will eat a lot of food, or binge, and then force themselves to throw up, or purge. The misuse of diuretics or laxatives also fits into this category.

Bulimia nervosa may sound similar to binge/purge type anorexia. Someone is categorized as having binge/purge anorexia and not bulimia primarily because of low body weight. There are other criteria for being diagnosed one or the other that will be covered later in this book. It is also important to note again that diagnosing eating disorders is very difficult, and someone with an eating disorder may develop behaviors that are part of other disorders as his or her disease gets worse.

tendencies, and this gives further explanation for the high number of suicides of those with anorexia. Sometimes people with anorexia are also perfectionists or obsessive and compulsive about behaving in the right way or doing the correct things. They may be diagnosed with other disorders, of which these actions are features.

What Is Bulimia Nervosa?

Vomiting after a meal—purging—is a major factor in another eating disorder called bulimia nervosa. Like those with anorexia, people with bulimia are depriving their bodies of important nutrition as a way to try to control weight. However, unlike those with anorexia, people with bulimia are often a normal, healthy body weight. It can be easier to hide the severity of the disease.

People with bulimia nervosa are caught in a scary, terrible cycle of bingeing and purging. First, they will eat an unusually large amount of food, often very quickly. Everyone overeats sometimes, but in psychological terms, a binge includes feeling out of control of what you are doing. When a binge is over, people with bulimia often feel a great sense of shame, fear, and disgust toward themselves. They will try to compensate, or "pay for," the large amount of food they ate. Many people know that sufferers of bulimia may make themselves throw up after a meal. In order to rid the body of the excess calories, someone with bulimia may also misuse laxatives or diuretics. He or she may also fast, which means not eating for a long time. Some purge by exercising a lot—as much as several hours a day. They will become upset if they cannot exercise and rarely take a day to rest from their workout routine. They may feel they have to earn food by exercising a certain amount. This is sometimes called exercise bulimia or compulsive over-exercise. Compulsive means a person cannot help doing something.

A person with bulimia does not binge because he or she is very hungry, but because of psychological problems, such as depression or anxiety. Just like people with anorexia, people with bulimia fear weight gain, but they generally are not unusually thin and do not look starved. Nevertheless, they, too, can be very unhealthy.

Hayley (full name withheld for privacy) always thought she was fat, even though she was 5 feet (1.5 m) tall and 125 pounds (56.7 kg). This is in the normal range, according to the body mass index (BMI), which is a way to compare a large group of people's weight to one another. When she was in the 10th grade, she tried vomiting for the first time after going on a diet did not work. She was not losing weight quickly and was hungry all the time. One day, she said, "I went crazy eating too much food!" Hayley forced herself to vomit. She remembers, "It was scary, but I felt relieved. I figured this is great because I can eat whatever I want, and I can just throw it up later!"[7] Soon, Hayley was vomiting up to five times a day, and it became easier and easier to do.

*Many people with bulimia binge in secret because they feel ashamed of their
eating habits.*

Most people with bulimia force vomiting by sticking a hand or fingers down their throat to make themselves gag. However, as time goes by, many can vomit at will. Most, like Hayley, vomit several times a day and both binge and vomit in secret. Despite their fear and shame about their behavior, like those with anorexia, those with bulimia are unable to control their disordered eating patterns. They suffer from depression, self-hatred, and an overwhelming dislike of their bodies. They often know that their bingeing and purging is unhealthy but continue the behavior because of a fear of weight gain. They resist facing the true dangers of their disease. These dangers may not be as severe as the dangers of anorexia, but they are very real. The longer the bulimia continues, the more likely sufferers are to develop medical problems and even life-threatening complications.

Bulimia affects 1.1 to 4.2 percent of all women. It is the second most common eating disorder among teens, and about 1 to 3 percent of teens suffer from it in the United States each year. Most people with bulimia are teens or young women. Only about 5 to 15 percent of those with bulimia are male, although it is likely that number is low due to men and boys not reporting their problem.

People suffering from bulimia may not look like they are starving, but their eating patterns are so disordered that they are putting their bodies in great danger.

Bulimia's Medical Issues

All eating disorders cause health problems, and bulimia can have serious consequences. Because of vomiting, many of these occur in the mouths of people with bulimia. Dental problems are common for people who purge by vomiting regularly, and the majority of those with bulimia have cavities and teeth that are breaking down. This happens because the acid in the vomit eats away the tooth enamel. Many victims have scrapes and calluses on the back of the hand they use to trigger vomiting. The salivary glands in the mouth often get bigger, and a person with bulimia may have puffy cheeks as a result.

Bulimia's Warning Signs

If someone with bulimia does not look sick or overly thin, how can you tell if a friend or family member is in trouble? Here are a few things to look for if you are worried about someone close to you. They:

- seem to eat an abnormal amount of food very quickly, or there is evidence they have done so (empty bags and containers—these may be hidden)

- frequently visit the bathroom after meals or smell of vomit

- often leave behind wrappers for diuretics or laxatives

- are deeply worried about a missed workout and continue to exercise even if they are tired, sick, or hurt

- have discolored teeth

- have calluses, or hardened skin, on the backs of their hands from purging

- are overly concerned about weight loss and seem to try to control food and weight

If someone you know is showing several of these signs, it is time to tell a trusted adult what you suspect.

At least half of those who have bulimia become dehydrated, which means they do not have enough water in their body. When someone with bulimia vomits or abuses laxatives or diuretics, they lose water as well as the food in their digestive system. They may also have an electrolyte imbalance.

Like those with anorexia, those suffering from bulimia risk heart problems, irregular heart rhythms, and heart failure. They may tear their esophagus from the strain of constant vomiting. In addition, people with bulimia may be constipated, which may be one reason their stomachs often bloat. These concerns can lead to life-threatening situations. Their stomachs may burst from a large binge, and this medical emergency often causes death. However, the danger of death generally is not as severe as it is with anorexia.

Binge Eating Disorder

Bulimia and anorexia share several symptoms, including depression and poor body image. Both kinds of eating disorders are extreme reactions to a fear of weight gain and fat, and both may include abusing exercise. Sometimes, people with bulimia fast and in other instances, people with anorexia may purge. Another kind of eating disorder involves bingeing without purging. It is known as binge eating disorder, and it may be the most common of all the eating disorders. It seems to affect males and females about equally and occurs in about 2 to 5 percent of Americans. Research shows it occurs more often in adults than in teens or young people.

Binge eating, according to the NIMH, includes several factors. First, those with binge eating disorder frequently eat a lot of food in a short period of time. They eat very quickly and eat until they are so full they are physically uncomfortable. Next,

Exercise Bulimia Unveiled

Exercise is great for the body. So more must be better—right? Like many things, exercise can be overdone. Those who already have a disordered relationship with food or other psychological issues are two groups likely to take exercising to the extreme.

Kiera Aaron wrote for *Shape* magazine in 2016 about her eating disorder, which included exercise bulimia. Each day, she would tally the calories of the food she ate in order to exercise appropriately later and burn them off. She wrote:

> I'd spend hours upon hours thinking about food—more specifically, how to either avoid it or burn it off. The goal was to eat 500 calories per day, often divided between a couple granola bars, some yogurt, and a banana. If I wanted something more—or if I "messed up," as I called it—I'd need to do cardio until I hit my net max of 500 calories.[1]

Looking back after getting treatment for an eating disorder, Aaron knows that her over-exercise wasn't about getting more fit. It was about dealing with the stress of her life, including her parents' divorce and a difficult relationship with her boyfriend.

Justin Sedor also chose to write online about his compulsion to exercise when losing weight. Sedor, who was overweight as a child and teenager, wrote that when he first started exercising and losing weight, he felt accomplished and proud. However, when he was no longer overweight, he continued exercising a lot so he could compensate for his eating habits. He started to binge and follow up the excessive eating with intense bouts of exercise. Years later, Sedor wrote that he saw that his "preoccupation with calories was getting in the way of my own success, my own sanity."[2]

Those who have bulimia are not the only ones to use exercise as a means to rid the body of excess calories. Experts report people with anorexia and other eating disorders do it, too. Some believe it is a big enough problem to become its own diagnosis in the future.

1.   Kiera Aaron, "What It Feels Like to Have Exercise Bulimia," Shape, February 12, 2016. www.shape.com/lifestyle/mind-and-body/what-it-feels-have-exercise-bulimia.

2.   Justin Sedor, "An Eating Disorder No One Is Talking About," Refinery 29, April 13, 2014. www.refinery29.com/exercise-bulimia.

binge eating differs from just overeating because the person bingeing feels a lack of control over how, when, and how much he or she eats. That's why binge eating disorder is sometimes also called compulsive overeating. Finally, those with binge eating disorder feel shame about their eating behavior. There are also several other behaviors someone with binge eating disorder may engage in, including eating when not hungry and eating in secret.

Rae Earl, the author of *My Mad Fat Diary* who suffered from binge eating in her teenage years, described how she would eat multipacks of chocolate bars at once and hide the wrappers. She described how a binge felt in an interview:

> *It's gorging the senses ... Just think about it—the way food is packaged, the way you can unwrap it and your fingers can touch it and then you get into the biscuit [cookie] or the chocolate—there's something very beautiful about that.*
>
> *It's unwrapping something, it's having your eyes [tantalized] by this shiny thing, and then you eat this gorgeous, velvety, crunchy sweet thing. It's a multi-sensory act. It's literally consuming, but it's all-consuming as well.*

However, that good feeling doesn't last, according to Earl and others who suffer from binge eating disorder. "As a teen it was a diversion from what my head was doing, anxiety-wise. It was kind of medicating my head with Kit Kats, which sounds ludicrous—but it did work in the short term,"[8] Earl said.

While she binge ate, Earl gained weight. That is not always the case; people with binge eating disorder may be of normal weight, but they are generally obese. Along with obesity comes a serious risk of medical complications such as high blood pressure, diabetes, high cholesterol, and heart disease.

Difficult Disorders

People with binge eating disorder, just like people with anorexia or bulimia, are trapped by their emotions and their disordered responses to food. Their behavior is self-destructive, yet they cannot do anything about it, which is why eating disorders are

Binge eaters will eat more food at once than most people consider normal for a meal, and they will continue eating even after they are no longer hungry.

defined as both psychological and physical. Eating disorders can last many years and have lifelong consequences for those suffering from them. That is why some doctors and mental health professionals have dedicated their work to researching how and why eating disorders develop.

Who Is at Risk?

According to the National Eating Disorder Association (NEDA), 40 to 60 percent of girls between the ages of 6 and 12 are worried about becoming fat. Studies show this concern follows them through life. What causes these feelings to emerge—and what turns them into full-blown eating disorders? Why are teens at so high a risk for eating disorders? These are questions parents, teachers, and medical researchers have been asking as cases of eating disorders have risen around the world. There is not one answer. Instead, there are a number of biological, psychological, and social issues at work that come together in different combinations to cause people to develop eating disorders.

Eating Disorders in History

Anorexia, although poorly understood and believed to be rare, has been medically recognized and written about for hundreds of years. In 1694, in a British medical text, physician Richard Morton described two cases of anorexia, which he named "nervous consumption."

Throughout the 19th century, anorexic illnesses were occasionally described by doctors but never scientifically researched. Generally, the medical community continued to see the starvation disease as a very rare psychological problem and referred to the cause as insanity, hysteria, or unsound mind. It was not until the 20th century that anorexia captured the attention of the medical community and the public.

In the 1970s, American psychiatrist Hilde Bruch claimed that in the recent past, most professionals had learned about anorexia in medical school but had never seen a case for themselves. It was that rare. She went on to say that anorexia had "for the last fifteen or twenty years [been] occurring at a rapidly increasing rate." She explained, "New diseases are

Eating disorders can affect anyone, but young women have the highest risk.

rare, and a disease that selectively befalls the young, rich, and beautiful is practically unheard of. But such a disease is affecting the daughters of well-to-do, educated, and successful families."[9] Bruch and most professionals of that time saw anorexia as a psychological problem that was the result of low self-esteem and poor body image caused by a culture that demanded perfection in women. Perhaps because young people from poorer families could not afford to see a psychiatrist, Bruch did not recognize that the disease could afflict people from all classes and ethnic groups, but she did force the medical community to recognize the importance of researching anorexia and its causes.

Bulimia was even less well known than anorexia until the 20th century. It was not even recognized as a disease until 1979. Perhaps because people were generally of normal weight and kept their behavior secret, little is known about how the disorder was described in history. In the few cases that were medically described, bulimia was variously attributed to brain damage, intestinal worms, "hysteria," or "perverted appetite."[10] Not until the 1930s was bulimia recognized as an emotional illness or psychological problem, and not until the 1970s did the medical profession begin to report an increasing incidence of bulimia nervosa. Even then, it was defined as a special kind of anorexia caused by modern cultural pressure to be thin and beautiful.

Binge eating disorder also was rarely understood in the past. Although people with cravings for huge amounts of foods were written about in medical literature, no one saw binge eating disorder as a specific illness of extremes. It was not even recognized as an eating disorder until 1994. Before that time, professionals did not distinguish between obese people who were binge eating and those who were not, although many doctors did believe that overeating was a symptom of emotional problems and depression.

Risk Factors

There is no consensus, or majority agreement, about what the "causes" of eating disorders are. Instead, medical professionals identify several risk factors that can contribute to someone developing an eating disorder. It is important to remember that anyone can develop an eating disorder, regardless of age, gender, race, or economic status. These risk factors have been identified over a long period of time to show who would be more likely to develop an eating disorder.

For people with anorexia, the first and greatest risk factor is a person's sex. Since 90 percent of those with anorexia are women, simply being a girl puts someone at risk for developing the disorder.

Next, people with anorexia have been found to have certain personality traits. Low self-esteem and a need to be "perfect" all the time are two traits those with anorexia often share. They are often considered neurotic, which means they have feelings of fearfulness and anxiety frequently. In addition, people with anorexia tend to believe they do not have much support from their social group.

A third risk factor for anorexia has to do with dieting. Those who begin dieting behaviors at a young age are often at a higher risk of developing an eating disorder later. They learn to be afraid of gaining weight as children and carry that fear into their teen years and adulthood. People who have suffered from digestive problems—anything from frequent diarrhea and stomachaches to picky eating—from a young age are also at risk for anorexia.

Another risk factor specific to anorexia is participation in athletic competition or hobbies in which people need to maintain a low body weight or believe they need to do so. Ballet dancers and long-distance runners are examples that can fall into this category, as well as figure skaters, gymnasts, and models.

There are known personality risk factors for bulimia, too. Like those at risk for anorexia, those who are at risk for bulimia tend to have low self-esteem and are perfectionists. They often do not take peer rejection well, have a hard time maintaining social relationships, and may have poor social skills in general. Being impulsive can be a personality trait of those with bulimia, too. That means they might make decisions really quickly and without much thought.

Sufferers of eating disorders often feel anxious and worry about making mistakes.

All in the Family?

Some experts believe another risk factor of eating disorders may be family dysfunction. This can mean unhappiness at home, such as a parent's divorce or struggles between members of the family. These may or may not include struggles about food. They report that sufferers of bulimia may see their homes as full of chaos, filled with frequent arguments, and generally cold places that do not support them. Risk factors in families of bulimia patients may also include the push for high achievement, whether in school, sports, or finding achievement through having an attractive appearance. An emphasis is often placed on weight or body shape as well as how and what the people in the family eat. Children of obese parents may also be at risk for bulimia.

Like other risk factors, family dysfunction is not a direct cause of an eating disorder. Parents are not to blame for a child developing an eating disorder. Instead, unhappiness or trouble at home can play a role in someone developing an eating disorder.

The Trauma Risk

One family behavior, however, is known to be a sure risk factor in the development of eating disorders. Child abuse, both physical and sexual, can be a real risk factor for an eating disorder. These abuses are kinds of trauma. Trauma can also include the death of a parent or family member, verbal abuse, or even witnessing a very upsetting event. Trauma is a risk factor for many other psychological disorders, too.

In 2008, an Australian study of teens and adults with eating disorders found evidence of sexual abuse in one out of every two young women with bulimia. That is a high number compared to a one in five sexual abuse incidence in the Australian community as a whole. Binge-purge type anorexia also has been found to have a link to childhood sexual abuse and other types of trauma early in life. Disordered eating is the way victims of trauma try to cope with how they feel or control uncomfortable and scary emotions. When treated for eating disorders, trauma victims often need help with other disorders connected to their trauma as well.

Say Anything?

The *New York Times* Well Blog reported on a 2016 study that looked at the impact of parents' comments about their daughter's weight and her body satisfaction years later. The study found that any comments on a child's weight, regardless of the meaning behind it, led to eating disorders, bingeing, and other kinds of dieting behaviors that could be unhealthy.

In the study, more than 500 women in their 20s and 30s were asked about their parents commenting about weight and how they viewed their body now. Those who remembered any comment about their weight made by a parent were more likely to believe they needed to lose weight. It did not matter if the comments were made often or only a few times. As long as the young woman remembered the comment, she had been influenced by it.

Other studies have linked parents' encouragement of teens to lose weight to those teens having lower self-esteem, continuing unhealthy dieting behavior, and binge eating. However, when parents instead focus their conversations with overweight children on healthy eating, these dieting issues have been shown to be less likely to develop.

In Your Genes

Genes are the basic units of inheritance in the cells of all living things. They are packets of deoxyribonucleic acid (DNA) that code for how an individual grows and develops. In humans, genes are arranged into 23 pairs of chromosomes, with thousands of genes on each chromosome. Although most genes in humans are the same for everyone, variations in some genes can determine whether an individual is at risk for certain diseases or vulnerable to environmental triggers of diseases. Scientists have found evidence that this may likely be the case with eating disorders.

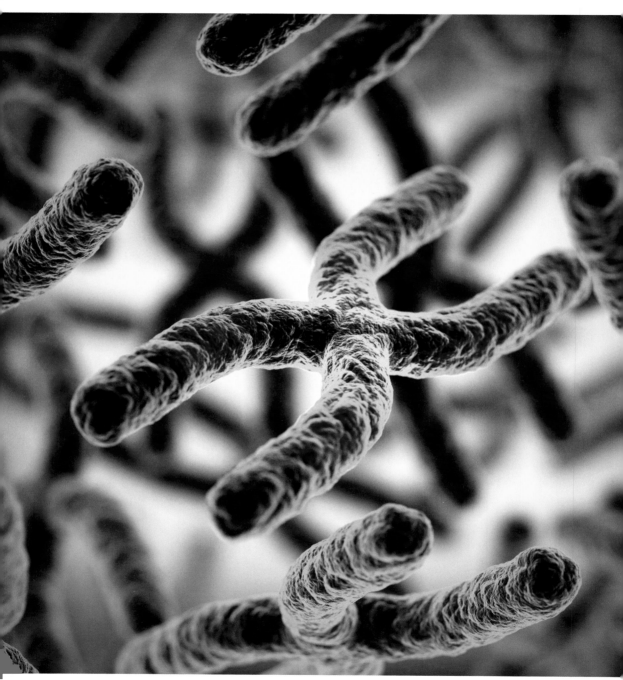

Scientists believe that genetics may play a role in the development of eating disorders.

People may be born with genes that make them more susceptible to developing eating disorders. This link is an important one. If there is a genetic component to eating disorders that means eating disorders can run in families. In fact, people with a family member suffering from an eating disorder are 7 to 12 times more likely to develop an eating disorder. Binge eating disorder, for example, seems to be inherited. One research team in Massachusetts studied the families of 300 obese people. Half of these people had binge eating disorder and half did not. The team interviewed family members and discovered that binge eating disorder was twice as common in family members of individuals with the eating disorder as it was in those who were not binge eaters. Anorexia and bulimia show the same kind of family pattern. One study demonstrated that family members are 8 times more likely to develop anorexia if one member already has the disease.

Studies of identical twins support a genetic risk for eating disorders, too. Unlike fraternal (non-identical) twins or siblings, identical twins have almost identical genes. Scientists have discovered that when one twin develops anorexia, the other identical twin develops the eating disorder about 60 percent of the time. In fraternal twins, this happens only about 10 percent of the time.

Scientists have searched for the specific gene that might be responsible, but so far, they have not been able to identify it with certainty. One gene that codes for reception of (picking up) certain chemical messages in the brain has been the most studied. Some studies found variations in this gene in those with anorexia, but other studies have not. Currently, scientists suspect that many genes are probably involved, but they do not yet know which ones. Bulimia seems to have a similar genetic component. Studies suggest that when one identical twin has bulimia, the other develops it about 44 percent of the time.

No one is doomed to get an eating disorder because of genes. Even if the specific genes that code for eating disorders become known, scientists still will know only about half of those at risk for eating disorders. After all, not every person with a twin who has an eating disorder gets an eating disorder. The other part of developing eating disorders is found in the environment, lifestyle influences, and personality. Scientists generally think about genes as predisposing a person, or making them more easily affected, to developing an eating disorder, but that something in the environment probably has to "pull the trigger."

In the Brain

Today, scientists and medical experts recognize that many factors may contribute to the development of binge eating disorder, anorexia, and bulimia. However, modern research suggests that these eating disorders might actually be brain disorders caused by changes in the chemicals and/or the wiring in the brain that control information about appetite and eating behavior.

The Risk Factor of Growing Up

In 2007, psychologist Kelly Klump at Michigan State University reported that puberty seems to be a major risk factor in the onset of eating disorders, particularly anorexia and bulimia. Klump studied 510 female twins and examined the onset of their eating disorders. By mathematically analyzing when an eating disorder started and what happened with the other twin, she was able to conclude that eating disorders that began before puberty were caused by environmental factors. However, once puberty began, she said, genetic predispositions seemed to be activated, and onsets of eating disorders dramatically increased in both sets of twins. As has been found with other studies, she reported that genetic influences seemed to be about 50 percent of the cause of eating disorders after puberty. Puberty is a time when dramatic chemical and hormonal changes take place as bodies grow to adulthood. Some scientists suggest these chemical changes may activate the genes that predispose people to eating disorders.

By studying twins, Kelly Klump was able to conclude that genetics plays a role in eating disorders that start after puberty.

Neurotransmitters and Hormones

Chemicals that help the brain send messages from one part to another are called neurotransmitters. One neurotransmitter is serotonin. Serotonin's job is to regulate mood, appetite and the way we eat, as well as controlling impulses. Many people with eating disorders have problems with the serotonin systems of the brain. Since the 1990s, studies have shown that people with anorexia have increased serotonin activity. Scientists believe that this disturbance in serotonin increases levels of anxiety and decreases appetite.

In 2005, one group of researchers suggested that restricting food helps to lower anxiety by decreasing the high serotonin activity in the brain. So, since those suffering from anorexia feel better when they are less anxious, they are encouraged to eat less and less. Therefore, although this serotonin problem does not directly cause anorexia, it may make a person more vulnerable to the disorder. Not all the scientific studies of people with anorexia support this idea, though. Some studies suggest that serotonin levels are decreased in the brains of those with anorexia as a result of malnutrition, leading to depression and a loss of appetite.

People with bulimia also may have disordered serotonin systems. Many researchers speculate that decreased serotonin activity in people with bulimia alters their mood, causes depression, and makes them feel the need to binge.

Another neurotransmitter, dopamine, may also have something to do with the development of eating disorders. Dopamine is involved in mood, attention, appetite, and learning. Researchers have discovered that when brains make too much dopamine, people can become obsessive, perfectionist, and worried. Too little dopamine can be associated with depression and an inability to enjoy experiences such as good food.

The more scientists learn about neurotransmitters and eating disorders, the more they suspect that many chemical changes are involved in the diseases, though none of it is fully understood yet. However, neurotransmission is not the only brain function that may be involved in eating disorders.

Chemical Synapse

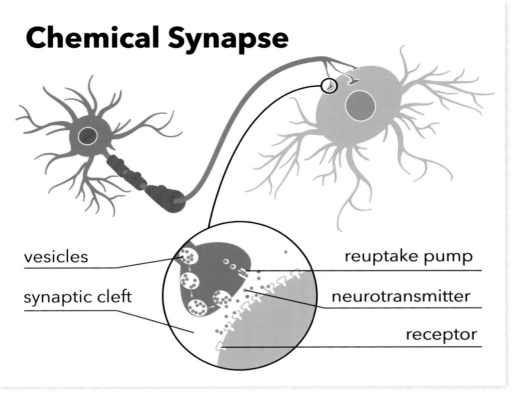

vesicles

synaptic cleft

reuptake pump

neurotransmitter

receptor

Synapses in the brain release neurotransmitters that control emotions and bodily functions. One theory for the cause of eating disorders is that the brains of sufferers of anorexia or bulimia release too much of certain neurotransmitters.

The hypothalamus is a small structure in the brain that plays a role in emotions (including releasing neurotransmitters such as serotonin), appetite, and sleeping, as well as producing hormones. Hormones are chemicals that control many body and brain functions. One hormone, known as cortisol, is a stress hormone and prepares the body to deal with threats and danger. Cortisol also decreases or turns off appetite. This works well for short-term dangers, but when cortisol is high for a long time and does not rise and fall normally, loss of appetite and depression can occur. Scientists have found that stress hormones, particularly cortisol, are chronically elevated in people with anorexia and bulimia.

Another hormone called leptin is produced by the body's fat cells. It travels to the brain and is responsible for signaling the hypothalamus either to send out hunger signals or to recognize fullness after a meal. Leptin has been shown to be low in people with anorexia and bulimia. It has also been shown to be defective in people with obesity. Although people may have normal amounts of leptin in their blood, the signaling of fullness to the brain has been shown to work inadequately in both obese people and in people with binge eating disorder. Such people may not know how it feels to be full.

Brain Circuits

The ways that different areas and pathways of the brain respond to stress also may be involved in eating disorders. One 2009 study compared the brains of 20 women with bulimia to 20 healthy women as they performed a frustrating, complex task. While the women worked, the researchers watched their brains in action using functional magnetic resonance imagery (fMRI), which is a medical technique that allows scientists to measure the amount of blood flow in specific areas of the brain. Using a computer readout, researchers can see a detailed picture of the brain as it is working. In this study, the brains of the healthy women showed activation and increased blood flow in the areas responsible for self-control, self-regulation, and focusing attention. These brain areas activated much less in the women with bulimia. They responded impulsively to the task and made many more mistakes. The researchers concluded, "Self-regulatory processes are impaired in women with [bulimia nervosa], likely because of their failure to engage [brain] circuits appropriately." They speculate that this problem with self-control "may contribute to binge eating and other impulsive behaviors in women with [bulimia nervosa]."[11]

Studies such as this fMRI exploration are just the beginning in the attempt to understand how brain differences can cause eating disorders. Much more research needs to be done before scientists can know for sure the many biological factors involved in the development of all the eating disorders. Even then, a large

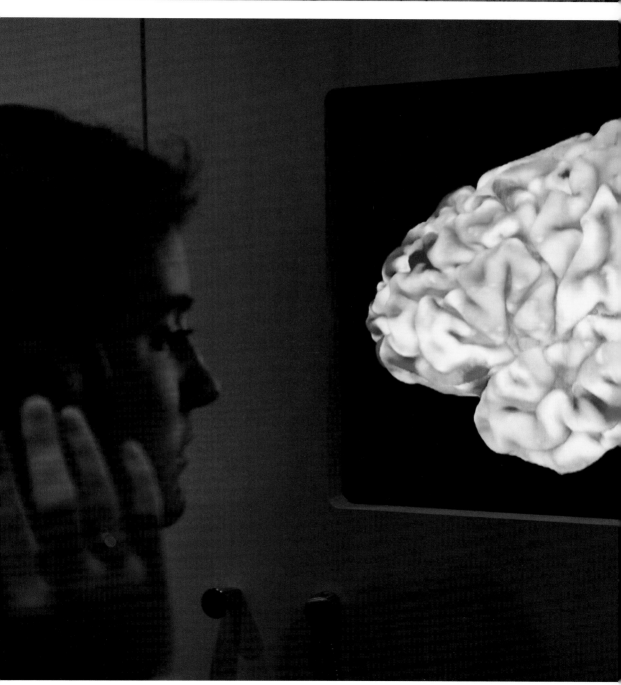

Researchers can use technology such as fMRI to see how the brains of sufferers of eating disorders behave differently than the brains of non-sufferers.

question remains: What causes these brain differences in the first place? That leads many experts back to genetics.

It is clear that there are many biological risk factors that can be part of why someone develops an eating disorder. However, these often are not enough to bring about an eating disorder on their own. Social and cultural risk factors, which can also be called environmental risk factors, are also a big part of the development of eating disorders.

COMPLEX COMBINATION

"I am relieved to know that this disease is not my fault, rather a complex combination of cultural influences, but more importantly those of genetics and brain chemistry."
—Mia Prensky, sufferer of bulimia

Mia Prensky, "Bulimia on the Brain," Serendip, Bryn Mawr College, April 18, 2007. serendip.brynmawr.edu/exchange/node/371.

CHAPTER 3

The Thin Ideal

Comparing yourself to other people is a part of daily life. You might ask yourself if someone is smarter than you because they got a better grade on a test. Or you might worry your friend likes someone more than you because they are funnier. Have you ever looked at another person and thought, "I wish I looked more like them?" Maybe you think they have pretty hair or a nice smile. It is likely you have even wished your body looked more like someone else's—perhaps thinner, curvier, or taller.

It seems like the media decides what is attractive for everyone—even if it is a tough standard for any regular person to live up to. Some people start to believe that their value is determined by their appearance, including what their body looks like. Social and cultural beauty standards, whether created by the media, looking at Instagram, or by peer pressure, are other risk factors for that can lead to someone developing an eating disorder.

THE MEDIA'S ROLE

"I do not believe the fashion industry or media cause eating disorders. Nevertheless, unrealistic standards, heavy photoshopping and lack of body diversity is a problem, and can trigger vulnerable individuals to pursue unhealthy behaviors. When the media is focused heavily on promoting only one male and one female body type—far removed from the average person—it can send a message that we must conform to these ideals in order to be happy and feel accepted."

–Amalie Lee, Instagram personality

Diana Falzone, "Amalie Lee Documents Recovery From Anorexia on Instagram," Fox News, September 1, 2015. www.foxnews.com/entertainment/2015/09/01/amalie-lee-documents-recovery-from-anorexia-on-instagram.html.

Celebrity Culture

In 1910, tall women with a body that looked a bit like the number 8—including a corset to make the waist as small as possible—were considered the ideal body type. By the 1920s, shorter women with few curves were suddenly more desirable. In the 1930s, curves were back in, but only soft, slight ones. Just about every decade, the "ideal" woman's body has changed.

The "ideal" man's body has also evolved in the media, too. Movie stars of the 1930s, such as Cary Grant and Clark Gable, had muscular figures, but they had to be slimmer because cameras made them look bigger on film. By the 1960s, very thin young men were the ideal, followed by a very muscular bodybuilder type glorified in the 1980s.

Just like today, these ideals were exemplified by the actors and models who starred in movies and were splashed across magazine covers and movie posters. Just like today, people then wanted to look like these celebrities.

The media and celebrity culture cannot be entirely blamed for the rise in eating disorders in the past few decades. However, when added to other risk factors, the continuous emphasis put on certain body types and the value of body above all could contribute to the development of or worsen an eating disorder.

Regular people are not the only ones affected by the "perfection" of celebrities' bodies. In 2010, singer Demi Lovato revealed that she had been suffering from an eating disorder, as well as depression and other psychological difficulties, for many years. As a child, she had gone through periods of starving herself, cutting herself, and bingeing and purging as ways to deal with difficult emotions. Then, as she became famous through her TV and singing career, she felt a lot of pressure to look a certain way—thin and perfect all the time. She had to get professional help with her eating disorder and was eventually diagnosed with bipolar disorder, a serious psychological disorder that includes having very "high" moments and very "low" moments.

After she was treated for bulimia and started to live more healthily, Lovato began speaking out about eating disorders. When she appeared on reporter Katie Couric's talk show,

The idea of what the "perfect" body looks like has changed dramatically throughout history and will continue to change in the future.

Demi Lovato has spoken out about her eating disorder and struggles with mental health.

another celebrity was revealed to have had an eating disorder in the past—Couric herself. Couric said she suffered from bulimia from ages 18 to 24 as she was in college and starting her career as a TV reporter. Her sister also had suffered from an eating disorder. In an interview, Couric said, "Like a lot of young women, I was struggling with my body image and feeling like I wasn't good enough or attractive enough or thin enough ... It can be so difficult to embrace the body that you have if it doesn't fit with the ideal. Women get praised for being super-thin, so you keep striving to be that way."[12]

Insta-Celebrities

Sadly for those at risk for eating disorders, celebrities are not the only ones seeming to promote certain body types today. Social media, particularly the picture-focused Instagram and Facebook, has made stars of models, bloggers, fitness enthusiasts, and others. As teens scroll through images of their "ideal" bodies, the social pressure can build up and intensify feelings of unworthiness, despair over one's looks, and longing for ways to transform into these insta-celebrities.

In 2013, a group of researchers at American University in Washington, D.C., had 103 girls take a survey about their Facebook use and body image. They found that those who looked at photos the most were the least satisfied with their bodies and wished more often to be thinner. According to the editor of the journal in which the study appeared, this finding was important because of the connection between poor body image and developing an eating disorder.

Thinspsiration or Fitspiration?

Instagram and Facebook can be further problems for those already at risk for eating disorders or who already have developed them. Since the Internet has begun to connect people around the globe, smaller communities have formed, including ones involving "thinspiration" or "thinspo." The term combines the words "thin" and "inspiration," and it has been used in online communities as long as they have existed. It is often used today to mean pictures and tips for those looking to lose weight, especially those suffering from eating disorders.

One Instagram user, India Edmonds, joined the social media network when she was 14 years old and quickly began to use it for thinspiration. For six months, she took selfies, dieted, and found out about ways to lose more weight through others' Instagram posts. She eventually passed out at her house and had to be hospitalized. There, she continued to refuse to eat. She even continued to take selfies as she dieted even more without telling her doctors. Perhaps the scariest part of Edmonds's story is that she received many messages from other girls who wanted

The Singer Who Educated the Public About Eating Disorders

Until about 1983, almost no one in the general public in the United States had ever heard of eating disorders. Those who had heard of them were not really aware that eating disorders needed to be taken seriously. Even people who had eating disorders themselves often believed they were alone in their behaviors and had little idea of the dangers. This all changed when the popular singer Karen Carpenter died of anorexia in 1983. Suddenly the problem of eating disorders leaped into the public eye. Massive media coverage about her death and its cause scared people and forced them to think about the seriousness of eating disorders. Several celebrity sufferers came forward with their eating disorder stories and promised to seek help. Actresses Jane Fonda and Lynn Redgrave admitted to coping with eating disorders. Singer and actor Pat Boone admitted that his daughter had an eating disorder. Ordinary people, too, sought help for themselves or their loved ones with eating disorders. Many people say that Karen Carpenter's lasting legacy is the modern public's awareness of the dangers of eating disorders. Ironically, Carpenter had already sought help for her anorexia when she died. She was trying to eat and get healthier, but her heart had been too weakened by years of malnutrition to be cured.

Many people were not aware that eating disorders were a problem until singer Karen Carpenter died in 1983.

to look like her at her lowest weight. Hers was only one of thousands of "thinspo" accounts on Instagram.

NEDA, along with other eating disorder research and awareness groups, have been working with social media sites to take down thinspo images because they can truly be dangerous tools for those suffering from an eating disorder. In 2012, Instagram, Tumblr, and Pinterest all banned thinspo images from their social media networks. Instagram even banned the hashtag #thinspo as well as other related hashtags users created to find content to fuel their motivation for thinness. Nonetheless, the thinspo accounts are still around. In 2016, *Wired* reported that banning the Instagram hashtags did not work. People started using variations on the words and letting others know what those variations were so they could still connect with others in search of thinspo.

It is commonly suggested that thinspiration is not the problem—it is the cultural ideal that thin is better. Some people are actively working to change wishes to be "skinny" to wishes to be "healthy." "If you're talking about someone being too thin, it's keeping it within the same language. Change some of the dialogues ... not just taking the [thinspiration] images down, but putting out messages that will counteract the overall cultural continuum,"[13] Katie Heimer, the Community and Education Coordinator for the Multiservice Eating Disorder Association, told the *Atlantic Wire*.

Heimer's idea is a good one, and many people—including celebrities—are trying to promote philosophies such as "strong is the

Social media platforms make friends' photos more accessible and easy to view as a point of comparison. Viewing these photos may begin to feel, to some, like peer pressure to look a certain way.

Pose, Filter, and Photoshop

Perhaps the most difficult aspect of the social risk factors of celebrity and social media culture is that most images we take in are not true to life. If the looks of celebrities and others with large followings on social media seem impossible to copy, that is because they are. First of all, celebrities spend a long time being prepared for the photo shoots people see in magazines and movies. They may exercise more in preparation for a role. They have professional makeup artists and hairstylists, as well as people choosing clothing that looks good on them. It is easy to look your best when you have professional help. In addition, the celebrities' poses and the lighting around them are carefully chosen by the photographer to make them look great. Lastly, it has been openly publicized for years that most magazine covers and other professionally taken photos are "perfected" in the Photoshop computer program. Wrinkles are removed, waists are made smaller, and legs are made longer and slimmer. Celebrities such as Zendaya have begun speaking out against this practice, sometimes saying they do not even recognize themselves after the changes are made.

Anyone who knows the tricks can do this to his or her pictures. Instagram stars have access to photo filters to make their skin look brighter. They can pose in such a way that their waists look smaller or they seem taller. Most take multiple photos and pick the best one. They may even use Photoshop to change a photo.

To someone at risk for an eating disorder, this information might not help them see "thinspo," or just typical celebrity images, as frauds. For anyone looking to change the conversation about the cultural "ideal" of thinness—or fitness—it is important to know about and spread the word.

new skinny." Oftentimes, this also goes too far in overvaluing appearance. In some online communities, "fitspiration" has replaced thinspo. Images of runners, weight lifters, and other athletes replace those of ultra-skinny models and actresses, but their message can be just as dangerous to those at risk for an eating disorder. Though pictures of super-fit men and women might seem like healthier images for people to peruse, they still put forth an ideal body and can be part of the social risk factors at work in the development of eating disorders.

Beyond Social Media

Pro-ana and pro-mia (anorexia and bulimia, respectively) websites were first exposed in 2001 to the shock and concern of the general public. Following this reveal, many sites were taken down. Oprah even did shows about the topic. By 2010, it seemed most of this pro-ana and pro-mia talk had moved to social media websites such as Facebook. A June 2016 *Newsweek* article showed otherwise. Though there are fewer sites now, pro-ana and pro-mia websites are still very much around. Some directly reinforce and validate eating disordered behaviors and feelings. They show anorexia to be "an act of extraordinary willpower."[14] Medical professionals worry that seeking out and visiting these

INSPIRATION OR SHAMING?

"If these images and messages categorized as 'fitness inspiration' actually inspire body shame—you feel ashamed of the beauty ideals you cannot reach and want to hide or judge your body or covet other women's bodies—then these messages are not inspirational at all. They trigger you to feel anxiety, hopelessness, and ask you to resort to extremes to get somewhere largely unattainable for healthy people."

—Lexie Kite, co-founder of Beauty Redefined

Lexie Kite, "'Fitspiration': Why It Isn't So Inspirational," *Huffington Post*, May 17, 2012. www.huffingtonpost.com/lexie-kite/fitspiration-isnt-inspirational_b_1524706.html.

websites can trigger eating disorders or worsen already existing disorders. They are yet another piece of the social and cultural risk factors of eating disorders.

A Sense of Community

There are experts who have watched the movement of pro-ana and pro-mia content move from message boards to online journaling sites to blogs and now to social media—but they see a silver lining. They argue that those with eating disorders turn to thinspiration sites and pro-ana or pro-mia social media for a sense of community. The messages presented on these blogs and websites are from eating disorder sufferers to others with eating disorders. They may be ways for those with eating disorders to express themselves among an understanding group where they feel accepted. As one *Slate* article put it: "Pro-ana blogs are easier to understand when you stop seeing them as propaganda organs and start viewing them as expressions of mental illness."[15] It also seems that placing restrictions on them, such as taking down thinspo sites and banning hashtags, only make the groups that follow them more secretive and tight-knit.

Some experts see social networking and website communities of those with eating disorders as invaluable for learning more about the disorders. Because eating disorders tend to begin in secret and many of the behaviors are hidden, it can be hard to know the thoughts, emotions, and actions of those suffering from eating disorders. As one writer said: "The scariest pro-ana message may be the one we can't hear: The Snapchat thinspo that dissolves before parents and press find it, or the WhatsApp group that organizes fasts where Google searchers can't follow."[16]

There is a very fine line between websites that promote starvation and bingeing and purging and those that offer a place for sufferers of eating disorders to commiserate while in a dark part of their life. In fact, research has been done to support both sides. It is another question about eating disorders that has not been fully answered yet.

It is nearly impossible to take ourselves out of culture and all social situations. That means it is nearly impossible to avoid the social and cultural risk factors for eating disorders. The social

Some experts believe that pro-ana and pro-mia websites can help sufferers of those eating disorders, but others disagree.

and cultural risk factors for developing eating disorders may be especially dangerous for teens who have grown up with the 24/7 world of social media that can be accessed with just the tap of a finger. Combined with family or peer pressure to diet, social risk factors such as very thin models or super-fit Instagram celebrities can certainly contribute to the development of an eating disorder.

Diagnosing and Treating Eating Disorders

Eating disorder experts can agree on one thing: The earlier someone with an eating disorder can be diagnosed and receive treatment, the better their chance for recovery. However, eating disorders often happen in secret or when sufferers believe no one is looking. Not everyone fits into a neat diagnostic category. Behaviors overlap between eating disorders as well as with other psychological disorders. These issues make diagnosis hard, and finding the proper treatment for someone with an eating disorder even harder. Furthermore, experts do not agree on what treatment is most effective. It may differ from one eating disorder—and one patient—to the next.

Therapy is an important part of eating disorder treatment.

59

Finding a Diagnosis

Before treatment can begin, an eating disorder must be diagnosed correctly. In the United States, eating disorders are diagnosed by medical doctors and mental health professionals such as psychologists and psychiatrists. They use a set of standards created by the American Psychological Association, called the *Diagnostic and Statistical Manual of Mental Disorders* (DSM). The DSM is updated every few years to include the newest research and treatment information available. It may change diagnosis criteria or names of disorders when it is updated. The current version is the *Diagnostic and Statistical Manual of Mental Disorders, Text Revision* (DSM-V-TR). This manual contains the criteria for identifying a wide variety of disorders of thoughts, feelings, and behaviors. Currently, the DSM-V-TR is generally agreed to be the best tool available for recognizing and labeling mental and emotional problems. The DSM-V-TR includes a section called feeding and eating disorders. As a group, these are defined as disorders in which eating or eating-related behavior is continuously disturbed so much that a person cannot take in and absorb the nutrients in food normally, resulting in health or psychological problems.

The *DSM-V-TR* recognizes four major classifications, and one other classification, of eating disorders: anorexia nervosa, bulimia nervosa, binge eating disorder, other specified feeding or eating disorder (OSFED), and one used in special situations called unspecified feeding or eating disorder.

Diagnosing Anorexia Nervosa

In order to be diagnosed with anorexia, a person must display three main criteria. First, the patient must have a low body weight for his or her age, sex, health, and growth and development. He or she must have achieved this low weight by taking in too little food through restriction of some kind. Next, the patient must also show a fear of weight gain or continue to engage in behavior that makes gaining weight difficult. Finally, an individual must have a distorted body image, including that he or she is unable to recognize how low his or her body weight is.

When diagnosing anorexia, doctors have to say whether it is the restricting type or the binge/purge type. In the *DSM-V-TR*, these are determined by how recently someone with anorexia has binged or purged. Someone diagnosed with restricting type anorexia will not have binged and purged within the previous three months and is more likely to be maintaining a low body weight by food restriction and exercise. The binge eating/purging type of anorexia is diagnosed when someone has been binge eating and purging within the last three months.

People with restricting type anorexia are likely to exercise too much as a way to keep their weight down.

In past editions of the *DSM*, anorexia could only be given as a diagnosis when a patient was below 85 percent of the suggested body weight for height, age, and sex. The *DSM-V-TR* gives guidelines for doctors trying to determine what "low weight" means in a patient. It tells doctors to consider how a child should be growing and whether he or she is meeting weight requirements for development. It suggests looking at a person's BMI. However, the manual also acknowledges that figuring out if a person's weight is low enough for diagnosis can be hard and simply tells doctors to consider the many factors that can be part of weight, including body build, weight history, and more. This recent change to the diagnosis of anorexia should be helpful in diagnosing more people with the disorder and catching it sooner.

Doctors make a diagnosis of anorexia nervosa by conducting a medical examination, interviewing the patient and family members, and by administering psychological tests that ask about eating behaviors and self-image. A doctor diagnoses anorexia only if the patient meets all the criteria listed in the *DSM-V-TR*.

Diagnosing Bulimia Nervosa

According to the *DSM-V-TR*, bulimia is characterized by binge eating followed by frequent purge behaviors to prevent weight gain, including purposely throwing up, fasting, over-exercising, and misusing laxatives and diuretics. It also defines what a binge looks like:

1. *Eating, in a discrete period of time (e.g., within any 2-hour period), an amount of food that is definitely larger than what most individuals would eat in a similar period of time under similar circumstances.*

2. *A sense of lack of control over eating during the episode (e.g., a feeling that one cannot stop eating or control what or how much one is eating).*[17]

In order to be diagnosed with bulimia, someone must be bingeing and purging in some way at least once a week on average for three months. Like the anorexia diagnosis, the

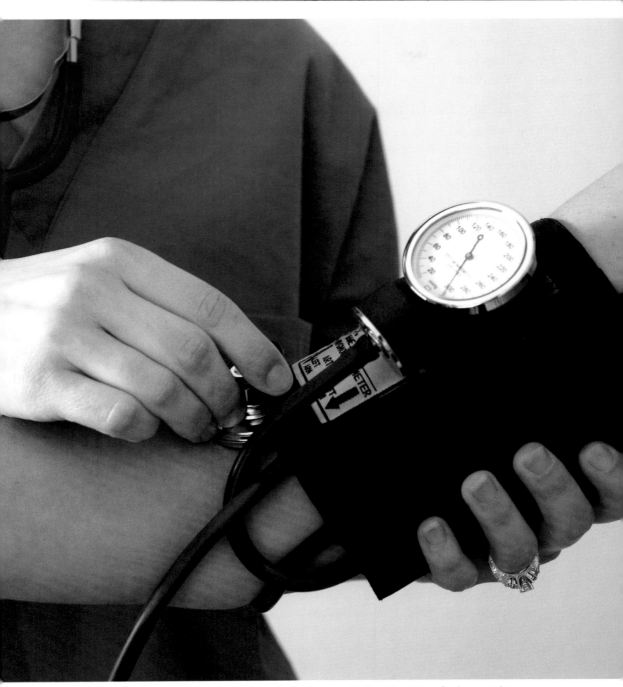

Before an eating disorder is diagnosed, other medical explanations for low weight or other problems, such as low blood pressure, have to be ruled out.

bulimia diagnosis also includes that the patient is very concerned with body weight and shape. Furthermore, before a bulimia diagnosis is given, anorexia of the binge/purge type should be ruled out.

Binge Eating Disorder

When diagnosing for binge eating disorder, doctors are looking for five traits in patients. The first is frequently occurring binge eating, which is defined in the same way as the bulimia diagnosis. The second has to do with what the binges are like. The periods of binge eating must have at least three of five characteristics: fast eating, causing a feeling of being too full for comfort, eating a lot when not hungry, feeling lonely and embarrassed by the amount of food being eaten, and feeling guilty and ashamed by the behavior. Next, patients must be upset about their binge eating. In a binge eating diagnosis, the binges are not followed by the kind of purging behaviors of other eating disorders.

The "New" Eating Disorder

Since the mid-1990s, another eating disorder has begun coming to light. Experts have named it orthorexia, though it is not a diagnosis included in the *DSM-V-TR*. Orthorexia is defined as being obsessed with eating healthy according to a set of guidelines, which can be different from person to person. Sufferers get very upset when they are not able to stick to their guidelines. They claim to strive for the best possible health, but often they lose weight from eating so restrictively.

The number of people dealing with orthorexia seems to keep increasing along with the numbers of other eating disorders. It may be part of the *DSM-VI-TR* if mental health professionals accept this diagnosis and can agree on a set of criteria for diagnosis by the time the new edition is published.

*Eating healthy foods is a good lifestyle choice, but when it becomes an obsession,
it can actually be harmful to a person's physical and mental health.*

Lastly, in order to receive a binge eating diagnosis, one must be bingeing at least once a week for three months on average.

Other Specified and Unspecified

OSFED is a diagnosis given to those who have disordered eating or dieting behaviors but do not fit the criteria given for the other eating disorders. With OSFED, doctors give a description as to why a patient is not being diagnosed with bulimia, anorexia, or binge eating disorder. For example, atypical anorexia nervosa is the description used for someone who is overweight or in the normal weight range but meets the criteria for anorexia otherwise. Descriptions also include bulimia and binge eating disorder of low frequency or for only a short time, and purging disorder, which does not include the binge eating aspect of bulimia.

Unspecified feeding or eating disorder is a diagnosis given when someone does not meet the criteria of another feeding or eating disorder. In this case, a doctor does not want to give a reason for why that criterion is not met. This diagnosis is also given in situations when enough information has not been gathered yet, such as in an emergency room.

Steps to Treatment

The longer an eating disorder lasts, the harder it is to overcome. According to the Cleveland Clinic's Disease Management Project, about one-third of patients recover completely, one-third greatly improve but still have some symptoms, and one-third continue to have an eating disorder.

Whatever the eating disorder diagnosis, recovery is most likely with early treatment and intervention. Ideally, it involves a team that includes a medical doctor, nutritional help, and talk therapy with a psychologist or other mental health professional. For young people, family therapy is also often used. The kind of treatment required depends on the severity of the eating disorder, the immediate medical dangers, and the patient's motivation to change.

Eating disorder treatment often follows a logical order:

- Take care of any immediate health issues, such as heart problems, dehydration, and low blood pressure.

- Decrease any risks that patients might harm themselves.

- Bring weight to a normal level.

- Stop bingeing and purging, and relearn normal eating behaviors.

- Identify and work on psychological and social issues such as low self-esteem, getting along with others, and body image.

- Maintain long-term recovery.

Health First

The top priority for treatment in patients with eating disorders is always medical treatment. This means immediate hospitalization for patients whose body weight has dropped to 75 percent of the minimum normal for their height and age or who have other dangerous medical issues. Those suffering from the effects of malnutrition or bingeing and purging may be given fluids through an IV. Medicines for low blood pressure and heart problems are given when needed. For patients who cannot eat on their own, a feeding tube might be threaded through their nose, down their esophagus, and into their stomach. They are fed liquids through the tube to give their body the nutrition it truly needs.

Because they are forced to eat healthy meals in the hospital, some people resist medical treatment. One worried mother, for example, remembers watching her teenage son with anorexia lying in his hospital bed "and trying to tear the IV out of his arm."[18] Another teen who was forced by her mother to see her doctor for her bulimia was furious. Her mother reported:

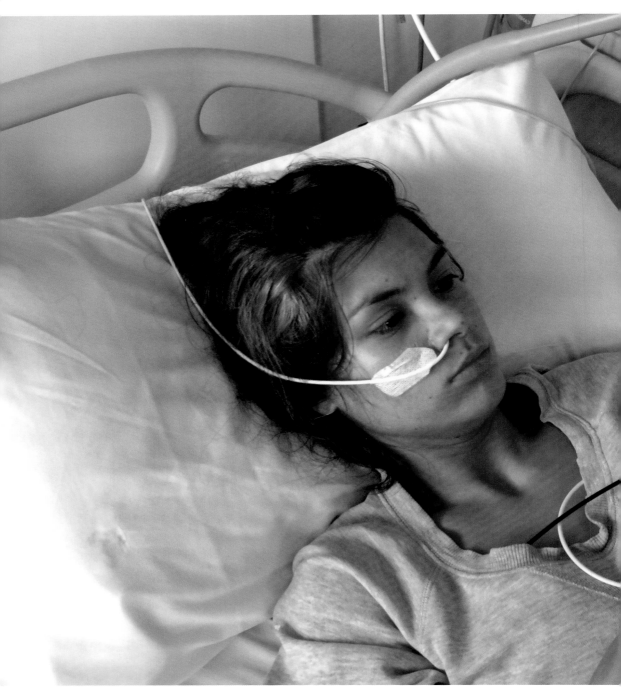

Sufferers of eating disorders who cannot or will not eat solid food in the hospital are given nutrients through a feeding tube.

On the way to his office, she urged me to turn the car around, claiming that she felt fine and that my worries about her health were "ridiculous." ... At one point, my daughter was madder at me than I'd ever seen her ... She was so riled up that I was afraid she'd open the car door and dash out.[19]

Eating disorder medical specialist Ira M. Sacker recalls meeting a young girl with anorexia just admitted to the hospital. The girl was screaming, fighting, and pulling her mother's hair. When Sacker had persuaded the teenager to calm down and told her she needed to be hospitalized, she "laughed and refused—totally, absolutely, adamantly."[20]

Fortunately, most people, no matter how much they resist at first, accept the need to be hospitalized within a few days. As they calm down and begin to feel better, they are able to cooperate with medical treatment. Then, once the patient is medically stable, he or she can be released from the hospital and the real treatment can begin.

A residential treatment center is a housing facility where people with eating disorders live together while they recover. At the facility, they receive daily therapy and other treatment.

Inpatient Treatment

For many people, treatment works best in a residential or inpatient setting. This can entail living at a treatment center for a period that may last from 30 days to as long as a year. One teen chose a residential institution called Canopy Cove when he needed to get help for his eating disorder. In this treatment center, he was removed from all the stresses and responsibilities in his life that were maintaining his anorexia. While he was a patient, he explained,

> I am in treatment all day, going through therapy and retraining myself to eat properly again … I have learned a lot in the first few weeks, but the process for my recovery is an ongoing, uphill battle. Canopy Cove allows you to step out of your normal comfort zone, challenging you to be free to experience new things. They use various methods of treatment to remedy the mind, body and spirit. These therapy techniques include music, art, yoga, and body image therapy and allow clients to enjoy the simplicities of life. I am beginning to understand my disorder and am starting to separate myself from it. The overall goal of recovery is to completely separate your mind and body from the disorder, giving individuals full control of their life.[21]

A part of Canopy Cove's treatment was nutritional. The center provided the healthy balanced meals that the young man's body needed. Part of the process was talk therapy in which he faced his emotions, insecurities, and fear of failure. Part of his treatment was educational. He learned healthy ways to handle his stress and how to continue his recovery after he left the residential center. It was a long process, but he did recover and today is an eating disorder activist, speaker, and writer.

The Cost of Treatment

Currently, many people with eating disorders must do without or struggle to get the kinds of treatment they need, even though they want to recover. Long-term therapy and residential programs are very expensive. While insurance companies are supposed to help pay for medical and psychiatric services, some have refused to pay for eating disorder treatment. The Academy for Eating Disorders issued a statement in 2009 that strongly opposed the insurance companies' stance.

However, their statement hasn't changed insurance coverage much. In fact, many websites offer parents and patients tips on how to fight for the full payment coverage many believe insurance companies should provide for those suffering from eating disorders. In order to receive the insurers' coverage, people may have to show proof of the eating disorder diagnosis and also show that the life of the person in need of treatment could be in danger without it.

Annetta Ramsay, the founding director of an outpatient eating disorder treatment program, wrote about her experiences working with families who are trying to pay for their treatment:

> Those of us who work with eating disorders can tell heartbreaking stories about insurance. I have seen families put second mortgages on homes or cash out retirement funds to cover treatment costs. Families tell me their out of pocket expenses for residential treatment start at $25,000, even when they are fully covered by insurance. For middle class families already facing eating disorders, the financial pressure can be too great, making aftercare that is critical to recovery unattainable.[1]

1. Annetta Ramsay, "Where Are We with Insurance for Eating Disorders in 2015?" Eating Disorders Catalogue, January 4, 2015. www.edcatalogue.com/insurance-eating-disorders-2015/.

Eating and Living Again

Residential centers can be the best treatment options for young people, too. One girl entered a residential center when she was 16 years old and was diagnosed with both anorexia and bulimia. She remembered,

> I didn't want to go to any institution … But the residential center I went to looked more like a comfy house than a hospital—that part I liked. I felt that everything I did there was under a microscope and monitored by staff—that part I didn't like. My days were organized around group meetings [where the patients could help and support each other], meetings with therapists, academic classes, and meals. Art therapy was part of the program as well.[22]

At first, she found the regimen very difficult. She said,

> I felt torn apart about doing what I'd vowed I'd never, ever do—gain weight. And there was no doubt in my mind that I was the fattest patient there and that if I started to eat, I'd never be able to stop … After eating, I'd feel that parts of me were inflating like a balloon, and that was upsetting—at times, almost more than I could handle. Sometimes I wanted to vomit, and I knew some tricks to use … but I didn't think I could succeed without getting caught.[23]

Like many in inpatient treatment centers, this young woman was eventually able to share her fears with the nurses and therapists at the center. She said that they helped her develop ways to deal with her bad feelings. As she got healthier, the day came that she began to believe she could get well. She began to trust in herself and her treatment and began to feel hope for the future.

Family-Based Treatment

Not everyone needs residential treatment for an eating disorder. Many people receive outpatient treatment. Some people "graduate" from a residential center to outpatient treatment. Outpa-

A GRATEFUL PATIENT

"To all the parents reading this, who are struggling
to find their sons and daughters trapped in a body
overtaken by an eating disorder ... KEEP GOING.
Your child may not be able to tell you right now,
they may not even realize it, but they appreciate
what you are doing more than you can know."
—Anonymous patient now recovered

Anonymous, "A Letter From Anonymous," Patients Speak: Personal Stories: Letters, F.E.A.S.T. (Families
Empowered and Supporting Treatment of Eating Disorders), May 2009. www.feast-ed.org/?page=M
ay2009Anonymous&hhSearchTerms=%22almost+and+year+and+before+and+let+and+touch%22

tients may have several appointments a week with therapists, nutritionists, and medical doctors, but they remain at home during treatment. For teens, family involvement often plays an important role in this treatment.

The best-studied and most promising approach is called the Maudsley Method, because it was developed at the Maudsley Hospital in London, England. Another name for this method is family-based treatment. With the Maudsley Method, parents play a major role in fighting the eating disorders. The parents are taught three phases of treatment behaviors. In the first phase, the parent is responsible for restoring proper meals and nutrition. Health, not gaining weight, is emphasized. The parent must prepare, serve, and monitor all the teen's meals and snacks.

After the teen is doing well with eating his or her meals, parents advance to the second phase of Maudsley treatment. They must now help the teen to prepare and/or choose his or her own meals and snacks. The parent still guides and monitors, but the teen has more independence and is trusted to try to eat normally. Once this phase is completed successfully, the family moves on to phase three. At this phase, they can begin to work on the feelings and problems in the teen's life that may have triggered the eating disorder. Parents have professional help throughout the phases of the Maudsley Method. The teen with the eating disorder is generally monitored weekly by a medical

Parents play an important role in eating disorder recovery.

Comorbidities

"Comorbidity" is a medical term meaning two or more conditions present in the same person. People with eating disorders commonly have other psychological issues occurring at the same time. According to the *DSM-V-TR*, the comorbidities of anorexia, bulimia, and binge eating disorder include depression, anxiety disorders, bipolar disorder, and alcohol or substance use disorders. In addition, many people with anorexia are also diagnosed with obsessive-compulsive disorder, and some with bulimia are found to have personality disorders.

Anxiety and depression are often deeply intertwined with the eating disorder. In fact, some experts believe the eating disorder to even be a symptom of other psychological issues such as these. Because psychological disorders are different in each person that has them, it's hard to know which disorder developed first. In an article in *Psychology Today*, one expert said people with eating disorders believe they can feel more in control of their anxiety, or fear (often of social situations), as they control what they do and do not eat. In addition, the act of purging has been shown to calm those with eating disorders. Also, feeling badly enough about oneself and life circumstances to develop depression can trigger an eating disorder. The feelings of hopelessness and shame those with eating disorders often have can trigger the development of depression.

When treating eating disorders, psychological comorbidities are treated, too. Many of the same treatments of eating disorders, in addition to proper medicine, are often used to treat anxiety, depression, and other psychological disorders. How much treatment and medicine someone might need depends on how serious the psychological issues are.

doctor and educated about the medical dangers of his or her eating disorder. In addition, the teen sees a nutritionist regularly to learn about food and health. A family therapist provides weekly counseling for everyone in the family.

Changing Thoughts

Many eating disorder experts use Cognitive Behavioral Therapy (CBT) as the main treatment for eating disorders. Rather than talking about difficult feelings and emotions, CBT stresses learning a different, healthy way of thinking and behaving. Typically, the CBT therapist may ask the patient to keep a daily log of everything he or she eats and to write down the thoughts or feelings that came with the meal. Then the patient and therapist discuss this record together and explore how disordered behaviors could be changed. They talk about healthy ways to deal with stress. They may also explore mistaken beliefs, such as someone with anorexia's opinion that he or she is too fat. The goal is to reduce and eventually eliminate starving, bingeing, or purging behavior. Some of the ways that CBT approaches eating behavior include drawing pictures of healthy bodies, learning facts about appropriate calorie intake, substituting binges with pleasant activities such as listening to music, talking about what

It Is Not the End of the World

During treatment for an eating disorder, relapses are common. A relapse is a return to disordered eating patterns after a period of improvement. Relapses seem to happen to about 80 percent of people during their recovery process. They are most common within the first six months of treatment. People who have been symptom-free for a year are often safe from relapsing. Relapses can be frightening and make a patient feel like a failure, but clinicians say that relapsing is not a sign that treatment is not working. It is just one step on the road to complete recovery. As treatment continues, the chance of relapse becomes less and less.

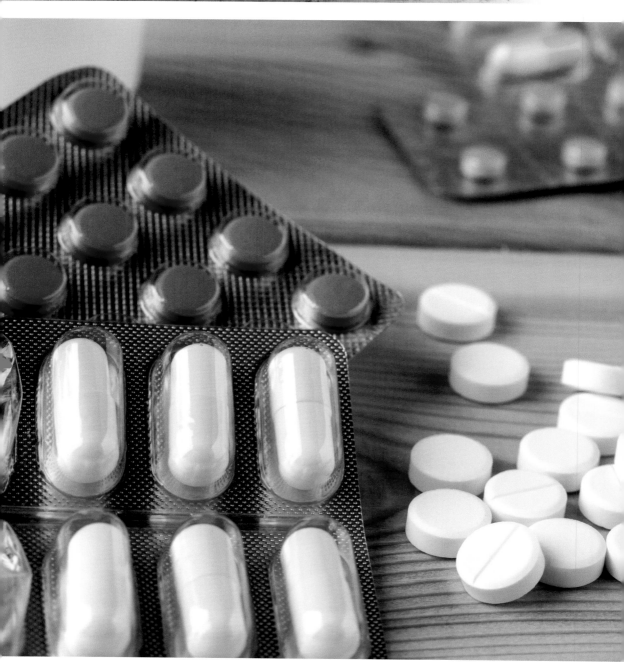

Because of long-term problems with depression and anxiety, many doctors prescribe medication as a part of eating disorder treatment. So far, though, one drug has not been proven to be effective for everyone in treating eating disorders.

makes people successes or failures, and studying the medical effects of disordered eating patterns. Even when the person cooperates and wants to change, however, the process can take a long time, even years.

No matter what the therapy or drug, treatment for eating disorders is never straightforward or simple. However, many people do find the courage and help to travel the long road toward recovery.

CHAPTER 5

Changing the Conversation

What if there were a way to stop an eating disorder before it started? Some mental health professionals and researchers are trying to find ways to do just that. They want to identify those who might be most vulnerable to developing an eating disorder through genetic testing and questionnaires. Others have created programs that can focus on groups, such as teenage girls, and offer help and education on the subject. This is called "targeted" prevention because it is aimed at the people who are most likely to develop eating disorders.

The medical methods of prevention are a long time away from becoming useful to the average person. Unless prevention programs come to schools or community centers, it is unlikely most teens have access to them. That is why some experts, celebrities, and general mental health advocates are working to prevent eating disorders by changing how we speak about people's bodies. They want our culture to value a person's character, work ethic, and intelligence more than his or her body—and they are not being quiet about it. While some people may develop an eating disorder regardless of social risk factors, this kind of "universal" prevention changes the conversation about weight and beauty in ways that could benefit them, as well as just about everyone else.

Prevention

If medical professionals could identify people who are likely to develop an eating disorder in response to stress, they could stop the problem before it begins. One way to do this would be to know the genetics that make someone vulnerable to eating disorders. NIMH has funded an ongoing genetic study of anorexia that began in 2005. Nine research facilities around the world are collecting genetic samples from 400 families that have at least two members with anorexia. At the same time that these people are receiving treatment, they also give blood samples and medical histories to the researchers. Researchers will compare the samples and look for specific genetic differences in family members who have anorexia.

With this knowledge, it will be possible for doctors to diagnose anorexia with a genetic test. This is important because medical doctors would be able to check for a vulnerability to

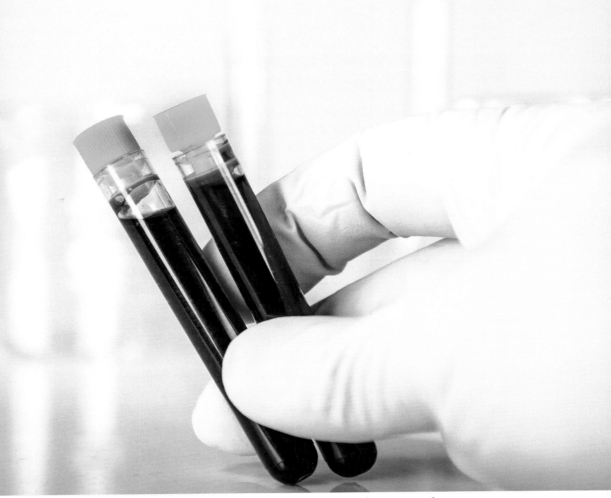

Analyzing blood samples helps researchers identify any genes that may put someone at a higher risk for developing an eating disorder.

anorexia at the first sign that someone has the disorder. Such knowledge might also help people to seek treatment earlier in the course of the eating disorder. Maria LaVia, a medical director at the University of Pittsburgh's Western Psychiatric Institute and Clinic explains, "Patients often blame themselves because they've caused this illness themselves by not eating or by eating and throwing up."[24] She believes patients and their families often resist seeking help because they are ashamed. LaVia hopes for a future in which no one feels at fault about an eating disorder. She works toward a time when long-term anorexia is prevented by simple, genetic diagnosis that leads to immediate treatment and early recovery.

WORKING TOWARD A GOAL

"The field of eating disorders (prevention, treatment, and research) is dynamic; it is always changing and growing in new and positive directions. Although knowledge has increased substantially over the last several decades, there is still a great deal to learn."
–David B. Herzog, Debra L. Franko, and Pat Cable, authors of *Unlocking the Mysteries of Eating Disorders*

David B. Herzog, Debra L. Franko, and Pat Cable, *Unlocking the Mysteries of Eating Disorders: A Life-Saving Guide to Your Child's Treatment and Recovery.* New York, NY: McGraw-Hill, 2007, p. 243.

Other researchers concentrate on the psychological or environmental factors that may trigger the development of eating disorders. These researchers look for specific ways vulnerable people can avoid disordered eating patterns. Though many risk factors for eating disorders have been identified, researchers continue to look for more specific risk factors. Finding more ways to test for risk factors, such as low self-esteem and amount of influence body weight and shape has on a person's emotions, can allow mental health professionals to more successfully identify who needs help.

Prevention Programs

Can risk factors be lowered if professionals target vulnerable groups of people with prevention programs? This was the question asked by psychologist Eric Stice and his research team. They concentrated on one risk factor, which they called "body dissatisfaction."[25] They wanted to test the value of targeted prevention programs for young women with high body dissatisfaction because they believed that this emotion could lead to eating disorders. The researchers studied 481 young women between the ages of 13 and 29 who were dissatisfied with their body shape and weight.

The women were divided into four groups and for a month in 2005; each group was in a different kind of program. One group was given psychological tests but not helped in any other way. Another group was directed to write about their feelings about weight, self-esteem, and body image. The third group was enrolled in a healthy weight class. These women learned how to eat more healthfully and to increase their exercise. They also kept food and exercise diaries. The last group participated in a "thin-ideal" intervention. They discussed and criticized attitudes about having to be thin to be worthwhile. They did role-playing exercises in which they had to talk someone out of "pursuing the thin ideal"[26] and explain why it was wrong.

Three years after the intervention programs, the researchers checked on how the women were doing. Some of them did develop eating disorders. However, those who learned about healthy weight or learned to question the thin ideal did better, with about 60 percent fewer cases of eating disorders than the other two groups. In addition, the group that got healthy weight information had 55 percent fewer cases of obesity (which can be related to binge eating disorder). The researchers had strong evidence that educational programs can prevent cases of eating disorders. They decided to use this evidence to develop an eating disorder prevention program that could be used in the real world.

Meet Them Where They Are

At the Oregon Research Institute, Stice and his research team developed the Body Project. It is a prevention program designed to reduce the risk of eating disorders in young people. Based on their studies, the researchers have included healthy weight education and education about the "thin ideal" that causes low self-esteem and poor body image. The project is being used in high schools and colleges around the country to attack eating disorders as well as the problem of obesity. It can be used to target people at risk or who feel at risk because they feel bad about their bodies and weight. However, it may also be used universally. Stice and his colleagues train high school and college teachers and counselors to lead the project in their schools. Body Project education includes learning about social attitudes that associate happiness with being thin. It involves role-playing and criticizing the thin ideal. The project includes learning to like one's body the way it is and then learning to eat healthily and exercise while discouraging diets.

After the educational part of the program is complete, participants engage in "body activism." They have to come up with "small nonviolent acts" that fight the idea that body size and shape determine self-worth. For example, Kelsey Hertel, a high school student in Oregon, completed the Body Project program when she was a junior. Then she and a friend made signs that read, "YOU ARE BEAUTIFUL. DON'T BE SOMEONE THAT YOU'RE NOT. BE YOURSELF." The girls posted their signs in all the girls' bathrooms in their school. Kelsey believes that her activism helps counteract poor self-image in fellow students who see the posters. She says, "They'd see the signs and say things like, 'That's encouraging because I always feel so fat and gross and ugly.'"[27]

Talking about the pressures society puts on people to look thin can help students identify and resist those messages.

How Should We Fight Obesity?

Scientists, doctors, politicians, and educators today say that the United States is suffering an obesity epidemic. They worry that excessive weight and obesity are a public health problem among young people that must be addressed. Advertising campaigns and school programs bombarding young people with messages about avoiding obesity and reducing calorie intake are just a few ways they are trying to fight obesity. Many overweight teens are being encouraged to go on a diet or exercise more.

While these recommendations are not harmful on their own, some eating disorder experts are deeply concerned that this constant warning about being overweight is causing an increase in eating disorders among vulnerable teens. Some may go on a diet that triggers anorexia. Others may be so determined to lose weight that they develop bulimia. Some may feel so discouraged and hate their overweight bodies so much that they binge for comfort and become obese. Social work expert Frances M. Berg warned, "An awareness is needed … that overemphasis on the risks of overweight can quickly escalate for vulnerable children into promoting thin mania, disturbed eating, and social discrimination [e.g., being bullied by classmates for being fat]."[1]

Are weight-loss programs aimed at children and teens doing more harm than good? A study of adults on a weight-loss program makes some experts worry. Researchers put a group of 50 obese adults on a very low-calorie diet, designed to produce quick weight loss at the beginning of the treatment. When that part of the diet ended and people were allowed to eat more normally again, 34 of them started to have binge eating episodes. They had not been binge eaters before the treatment started. Experts are concerned children might have a similar disordered eating response to going on a diet and that the problem could follow them through life.

1. Frances M. Berg, "Prevention Programs for Obesity and Related Problems," *Healthy Weight Journal*, vol. 15, no. 4, July/August 2001, p. 62. www.gurze.net/HAESprotected/HAES15-4.pdf.

PERFECTION SHOULD NOT BE THE GOAL

"There is a lot of negative messaging in our society. The biggest mistake we make is beating ourselves up for not looking like models or celebrities. It's time we stop emulating or striving for a type of perfection that doesn't even exist in the real world. It's OK to look like a human!"
—Caitlin Boyle, founder of Operation Beautiful

Robin Long, "Caitlin Boyle, Founder of Operation Beautiful," *The Balanced Life*, August 15, 2011. thebalancedlifeonline.com/caitlin-boyle-founder-of-operation-beautiful/.

Every Body Is a Good Body

Though the number of those with eating disorders seems to keep rising, people are pushing back on many of the social and cultural values that can become risk factors for developing an eating disorder.

Caitlin Boyle founded Operation Beautiful in June 2009 to combat negative thoughts she was having about herself. At first, it was just her posting notes in public restrooms with messages such as "You are beautiful" or "You are amazing just the way you are." She started blogging about her notes, and other people began to follow her example. Many people, including many young women, have used her movement to spread body positivity and end "fat talk." Boyle has gotten pictures of thousands of notes from those who have read her blog or books. She said they have been posted on all seven continents—even in Antarctica. Boyle now gives presentations around the United States about positive self-talk and how to work toward a less body-focused culture.

In an interview about Operation Beautiful, Boyle shared a story about a girl suffering from anorexia finding an Operation Beautiful note:

She was in an eating disorder treatment facility for anorexia and at a critical place with her illness. Her doctors were telling her she was going to die. She was losing her hair and getting [EKGs]; her life was crumbling.

She told me that when she went into the bathroom to throw up, she found an OB [Operation Beautiful] note on the stall door that said, "You're good enough the way you are," signed by OB.com.

She said that she has been told that by everyone, but finding that note, and knowing that it was written by a stranger, she took it as a sign from God or a message from the Universe. In her email to me, she wrote "I'm going to get better."[28]

Operation Beautiful is a movement that involves posting notes with body-positive messages in public places.

No More Models

Fashion magazines have been some of the worst offenders when it comes to using super-skinny models to showcase clothing. Fashion runway shows may be even worse. Both have responded to the wish for fewer models who were so thin that people feared for their health. The British Fashion Council called for models to be checked for eating disorders in 2007. In 2012, *Vogue* banned models under the age of 16 who appeared to have eating disorders. In 2015, France passed a law against hiring extremely thin models and set fines for images that were not labeled as having been altered.

These changes are not enough for many people. They argue that even models who are not underweight still promote bodies that are difficult for most people to attain. Calls for more "average" looking bodies have gotten louder in the last few years—and some companies have answered.

The young women's clothing company Aerie stopped retouching photos of their models in 2014. Its #aerieREAL photos also included young women of varying sizes and shapes. People buying the company's clothing responded strongly to this advertising campaign; by 2015, Aerie's profits had increased by 20 percent. In 2016, Aerie launched a new campaign that used "real" women in their clothing alongside the still-unretouched models. The women were many sizes, colors, and ages, and included in this group was Aerie's "official role model," Iskra Lawrence, who survived an eating disorder and now raises awareness for NEDA and speaks out about body positivity. It is clear that the diversity in the bodies in Aerie's campaigns still sells clothing—and maybe sells it better—than traditional advertising. Campaigns such as Aerie's could change advertising for the better.

Some countries have put restrictions on how thin a model can be. Critics argue that models promote unrealistic standards of beauty.

APPRECIATE YOURSELF

"I think no matter what you look like, the key is to first of all be happy with yourself. And then you know if you want to try to improve things that you don't like about yourself, then do it after you appreciate yourself."
—Adele, singer

"Celebrity Body Talk: Women Who Defy Conventional Body Types In Hollywood (Photos)," *Huffington Post*, January 24, 2013. www.huffingtonpost.com/2013/01/25/celebrity-body-talk-women-who-defy-conventional-body-types_n_2537034.html?slideshow=true#gallery/276504/10.

What About Boys and Men?

Even though women and girls are the majority of those with eating disorders, that does not mean they are the only ones who need the cultural values of "appearance over everything" to change. These social ideals affect men and boys, too. They have additional social expectations to deal with as well:

> Because we still live in a culture that demands that men remain unaffected by emotional issues and "man up," they have no space in which to safely talk about bullying, self-esteem, and other important body topics. Friends, silent oppression is the scariest oppression of them all.[29]

With this in mind, it is just as important that men and boys have advocates for body positivity as it is for girls and women. Furthermore, those who develop eating disorders need someone to speak for them when they are too ashamed to speak for themselves.

Andrew Walen blogs about eating disorders and particularly about men and eating disorders at The Body Image Therapy Center's website. He challenges the statistic about men being only 1 in every 10 people with an eating disorder. Instead, he says this only represents the men who are diagnosed with eating disorders and that the number is much higher. One reason he gives for why men are not diagnosed with eating disorders is

Men can also develop eating disorders, but their focus is generally more on becoming muscular than becoming thin, which can make it harder to diagnose them.

how these disorders show up: "body dissatisfaction in males is typically characterized by a drive for muscularity rather than a drive for thinness."[30]

Walen wrote in 2016 that men and boys are seriously underrepresented in research about eating disorders. He reported that only about 1 percent of eating disorder research is about men and boys. This makes treating their disorders more difficult.

He hopes eating disorder recovery centers and mental health professionals will work to target men with these issues more in the future. He addresses men and others who have eating disorders, writing that they must speak out for themselves, so they can be better represented in the future:

> It's not your fault that you have an eating disorder. But it is your responsibility to get help. You do it for you. You do it for your loved ones. You do it for your future. And hopefully you do it to help create a cultural shift that those with the dollars to help raise awareness on a large scale start to take note of people just like you who may not fit the typical model of an eating disorder sufferer.[31]

Take Care of Yourself

The Center for Young Women's Health at Children's Hospital in Boston offers these tips to teens for staying healthy and developing a good body image:

- *Write down things that your body can do when it's healthy (running, dancing, hiking, biking, etc.)*

- *Write down 10 qualities you like about yourself (caring, responsible, funny, smart, creative, etc.)*

- *Make a list of accomplishments you are proud of*

- *Buy clothes that you feel comfortable in and give away any that make you feel self-conscious or uncomfortable*

- *Relax using all your senses. Take a bath, listen to music, play a game, sing, or meditate*

- *Spend time with positive people who make you feel comfortable and you can be yourself around*

- *Remind yourself that everyone's body is unique and not everyone is meant to be the same shape or size*

- *Be critical of advertisements, magazines, and the media*

- *Make yourself smile when you look in the mirror. It might feel weird at first, but after awhile, you could start to notice a difference in the way you see yourself[32]*

These tips are an excellent starting place to develop a good body image and stay away from disordered eating. However, if you or a friend starts to feel unsatisfied with your body, begins to diet in a way you know to be unhealthy, or begins purge behaviors, it is not too late. You can always tell a trusted adult, such as a parent or teacher, or talk to your doctor. Those suffering from eating disorders may feel alone in their disorder—but they do not need to be.

Chapter 1: What Is an Eating Disorder?

1. Quoted in Lisa Flam, "Recovered Anorexic Inspires by Example," *Today*, September 30, 2015. www.today.com/health/recovered-anorexic-now-inspiring-others-example-t47091.

2. Quoted in Flam, "Recovered Anorexic Inspires by Example."

3. Quoted in Tess Koman, "This Woman Chronicling Her Anorexia Recovery on Instagram Is 'Damn Proud' of Her Weight Gain," *Cosmopolitan*, August 28, 2015. www.cosmopolitan.com/health-fitness/news/a45534/amalie-lee-instagram-anorexia-recovery/.

4. Quoted in Mike Mariani, "How Pro-Anorexia Websites Affect the Psychology of Eating Disorders," *Newsweek*, June 23, 2016. www.newsweek.com/2016/07/01/pro-ana-websites-anorexia-nervosa-473433.html.

5. "Eating Disorders," National Institute of Mental Health, February 2016. www.nimh.nih.gov/health/topics/eating-disorders/index.shtml.

6. Quoted in David B. Herzog, Debra L. Franko, and Pat Cable, *Unlocking the Mysteries of Eating Disorders: A Life-Saving Guide to Your Child's Treatment and Recovery*. New York, NY: McGraw-Hill, 2008, p. 30.

7. Hayley, "Hayley's Story," Eating Disorders in a Disordered Culture: Stories Told: Bulimia Stories, University of California Davis, eating.ucdavis.edu/speaking/told/bulimia/b77hayley.html.

8. Quoted in Emily Reynolds, "Binge Eating Disorder—What Is It and Where Can You Get Help?" *Metro*, July 28, 2016. metro.co.uk/2016/07/28/binge-eating-disorder-what-is-it-and-where-can-you-get-help-6031089/#ixzz4FuFoL36l.

Chapter 2: Who Is at Risk?

9. Quoted in Joan Jacobs Brumberg, *Fasting Girls: The History of Anorexia Nervosa*. Cambridge, MA: Harvard University Press, 1988, p. 10.

10. Brenda Parry-Jones and William L. Parry-Jones, "History of Bulimia and Bulimia Nervosa," in Kelly D. Brownell and Christopher G. Fairburn, eds., *Eating Disorders and Obesity*. New York, NY: Guilford, 1995, p. 149.

11. Rachel Marsh et al., "Deficient Activity in the Neural Systems That Mediate Self-Regulatory Control in Bulimia Nervosa," *Archives of General Psychiatry*, vol. 66, no. 1, January 2009, pp. 51–63. archpsyc.ama-assn.org/cgi/content/short/66/1/51.

Chapter 3: The Thin Ideal

12. Quoted in Associated Press, "Katie Couric Opens Up About Battling Bulimia," *USA Today*, September 24, 2012. usatoday30.usatoday.com/life/people/story/2012/09/24/katie-couric-opens-up-about-battling-bulimia/57837718/1.

13. Quoted in Rebecca Greenfield, "To Ban or Not to Ban: How Do You Solve the Problem of Thinspo?" *The Atlantic*, August 21, 2012. www.theatlantic.com/technology/archive/2012/08/ban-or-not-ban-how-do-you-solve-problem-thinspo/324471/.

14. Mariani, "How Pro-Anorexia Websites Affect the Psychology of Eating Disorders."

15. Amanda Hess, "The Panic Over Pro-Anorexia Websites Isn't Healthy," *Slate*, July 14, 2015. www.slate.com/articles/technology/users/2015/07/pro_anorexia_and_pro_bulimia_websites_blogs_and_social_media_moral_panic.html.

16. Hess, "The Panic Over Pro-Anorexia Websites Isn't Healthy."

Chapter 4: Diagnosing and Treating Eating Disorders

17. American Psychiatric Association. *Diagnostic and Statistical Manual of Mental Disorders* (5th ed.). Washington, DC: American Psychiatric Association, 2013.

18. B. Timothy Walsh and V.L. Cameron, *If Your Adolescent Has an Eating Disorder*. New York, NY: Oxford University Press, 2005, p. 129.

19. Quoted in Herzog, Franko, and Cable, *Unlocking the Mysteries of Eating Disorders*, p. 127.

20. Ira M. Sacker, *Regaining Your Self: Breaking Free from the Eating Disorder Identity: A Bold New Approach*. New York, NY: Hyperion, 2007, p. 3.

21. Patrick Bergstrom, "A Fallen Athlete," I Chose to Live, pp. 22–23. www.ichosetolive.com/files/A_Fallen_Athlete.pdf.

22. Quoted in Herzog, Franko, and Cable, *Unlocking the Mysteries of Eating Disorders*, p. 70.

23. Quoted in Herzog, Franko, and Cable, *Unlocking the Mysteries of Eating Disorders*, p. 70.

Chapter 5: Changing the Conversation

24. Quoted in Chuck Staresinic, "Refusing Sustenance: In Search of Earthly Explanations for Eating Disorders," PittMed, May 2004, p. 15. pittmed.health.pitt.edu/May_2004/cover_story.pdf.

25. Eric Stice et al., "Dissonance and Healthy Weight Eating Disorder Prevention Programs: Long-Term Effects from a Randomized Efficacy Trial," *Journal of Consulting and Clinical Psychology*, vol. 76, no. 2, 2008, p. 329. foodaddictionsummit.org/docs/SticeMarti2008.pdf.

26. Stice et al., "Dissonance and Healthy Weight Eating Disorder Prevention Programs," pp. 332-333.

27. Quoted in Sanjay Gupta, "Taking on the Thin Ideal," *Fit Nation*, CNN/*TIME*. content.time.com/time/specials/2007/article/0,28804,1703763_1703764_1810730,00.html.

28. Stacey Gualandi, "Caitlin Boyle Changes Lives With Her Operation Beautiful Movement," The Women's Eye, April 11, 2012. www.thewomenseye.com/2012/04/11/interview-caitlin-boyle-changes-lives-with-operation-beautiful-movement/.

29. Jes Baker, "7 Men To Follow In The Body Positive Movement," Ravishly, September 2, 2015. www.ravishly.com/2015/09/02/7-men-follow-body-positive-movement.

30. Walen, Andrew, "Males Don't Present like Females with Eating Disorders," The Body Image Center, May 24, 2016. thebodyimagecenter.com/news-blogs/men-with-eating-disorders-news-blogs/males-dont-present-females-eating-disorders/.

31. Andrew Walen, "We Have a Long Way to Go," The Body Image Center, May 09, 2016. thebodyimagecenter.com/news-blogs/men-with-eating-disorders-news-blogs/long/.

32. "Eating Disorders: General Information," Center for Young Women's Health, July 5, 2016. youngwomenshealth.org/2012/04/11/eating-disorders/.

Chapter 1: What Is an Eating Disorder?

1. How are eating disorders different from diets or unhealthy eating?

2. How are anorexia, bulimia, and binge eating disorder similar, and how are they different?

3. What are ways eating disorders can harm the body?

Chapter 2: Who Is at Risk?

1. Why can't one specific "cause" of eating disorders be described?

2. How do genetics and environment interact to cause eating disorders?

3. How do you think families could deal with the possibility of an eating disorder "running in the family"?

Chapter 3: The Thin Ideal

1. How might celebrity culture be a part of the development of eating disorders?

2. Do you see a difference between "thinspiration" and "fitspiration"? Why or why not?

3. Do you think there is a place for pro-ana and pro-mia websites? Why or why not?

Chapter 4: Diagnosing and Treating Eating Disorders

1. Why is diagnosing an eating disorder so difficult?

2. What is the Maudsley method, and why is it a good treatment approach?

3. What are the benefits of residential treatment versus outpatient treatment?

Chapter 5: Changing the Conversation

1. What are some of the benefits of prevention programs?

2. What are some examples of "fat talk," and why might avoiding such talk help prevent eating disorders?

3. What are ways boys and men can start to get better eating disorder help?

Academy for Eating Disorders (AED)

12100 Sunset Hills Rd.
Suite 130
Reston, VA 20190
Phone: (703) 234-4079
Website: www.aedweb.org
AED is a professional organization that emphasizes prevention and research.

Eating Disorder Referral and Information Center

2923 Sandy Pointe, Ste. 6
Del Mar, CA 92014
Phone: (858) 481-1515
Website: www.edreferral.com
This organization provides an extensive and searchable database about where and how to get treatment for eating disorders. It also answers questions about treatment and prevention of eating disorders.

National Eating Disorders Association (NEDA)

603 Stewart St., Ste. 103
Seattle, WA 98101
Phone: (800) 931-2237
Website: www.nationaleatingdisorders.org
NEDA provides education, resources, and support for those affected by eating disorders, as well as their friends and family.

National Institute of Mental Health (NIMH)
6001 Executive Blvd., Room 8184 MSC 9663
Bethesda, MD 20892
Phone: (866) 615-6464
Website: www.nimh.nih.gov
NIMH offers a wide selection of informational publications about eating disorders.

Books

Abblett, Mitch, and Christopher Willard. *Mindfulness for Teen Depression: A Workbook for Improving Your Mood.* Oakland, CA: Instant Help Books, 2016.
Teens who suffer from depression have a greater chance of developing disordered eating. This workbook can help them work through tough emotions and situations.

Dunkle, Elena, and Clare B. Dunkle. *Elena Vanishing: A Memoir.* San Francisco, CA: Chronicle Books, 2015.
Teens can learn firsthand the difficulties of having anorexia and how their life could change because of it in this memoir.

Lask, Bryan, and Lucy Watson. *Can I Tell You About Eating Disorders?: A Guide for Friends, Family, and Professionals.* Philadelphia, PA: Jessica Kingsley Publishers, 2014.
Talking about eating disorders is hard, but this volume aids everyone who may need to understand and discuss these problems.

Poole, Hillary W. *Eating Disorders.* Broomall, PA: Mason Crest, 2016.
This accessible overview of major eating disorders, their causes, and their treatment can help young readers better understand the main concepts of eating disorders.

Wilcox, Christine. *Teens and Body Image.* San Diego, CA: ReferencePoint Press, 2016.
A discussion of common body image issues, their causes, and how to improve these issues, this book can help teens deal with difficult thoughts and feelings.

Websites

The Healthy Teen Project

www.healthyteenproject.com/adolescent-eating-disorders-ca
Information, resources, inspiration, and more can be found here for those suffering from eating disorders or those caring for them.

Helping Other People Eat (HOPE)

www.hopetolive.com/eating-disorders.html
This nonprofit organization works to spread information about eating disorders through donations, speakers, and events.

KidsHealth: Food and Fitness

kidshealth.org/en/teens/food-fitness/
Articles include the basics of a healthy lifestyle, including nutrition and exercise information. In the section "Problems with Food and Exercise," visitors can learn about eating disorders, body image, helping friends with eating disorders, and more.

Operation Beautiful

www.operationbeautiful.com/about-2/
Spread the message of body positivity using ideas from Operation Beautiful.

Safe Teens: Body Image

www.safeteens.org/mind-body/body-image/
Read ways to improve body image on this website that caters to teen issues.

INDEX

Kristen Rajczak Nelson holds a BA in English from Gannon University and an MA in Arts Journalism from the S.I. Newhouse School of Public Communication at Syracuse University. She has written hundreds of books for children on a variety of topics, including character building, human body systems, and American history. She lives in Buffalo, New York, with her husband, a child psychologist.